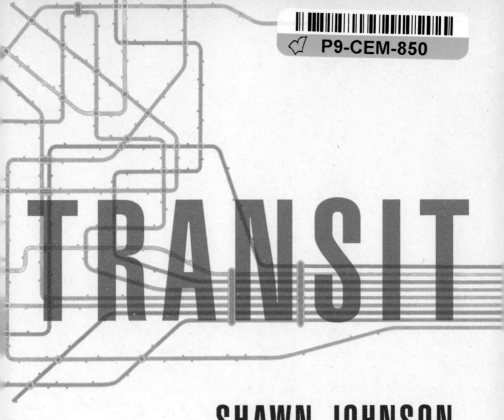

TRANSIT

SHAWN JOHNSON

B&H
PUBLISHING GROUP
Nashville, Tennessee

This is dedicated to Ethan, Austin, and Ashton.

These spiritual vehicles will change your life, boys! God loves you just the way you are. He has a special plan for each of you and wants to be close with you in a real way. I love you so much . . . that I don't even know how to fully express it in words, and as crazy as it is to me, God loves you even more!

THOSE WHO MADE THIS POSSIBLE

Mom: For everything you had to sacrifice when our journey together began, and your constant pursuit after God finally paid off with me.

Eric Parks: For believing in me when nobody else did.

Jeanne Mayo: For taking a risk on a messed up kid and encouraging me into the kingdom of God.

Jeremy DeWeerdt and everybody from Rockford First: For providing a place for me to learn how to pursue God and find a passion for making Him known.

Dad, Paul, and Lorrie: For being a supporting family as I've chased my dreams.

Chad Bruegman, Scott Bruegman, and Brian Zibell: For your partnership, your loyalty, your encouragement, your trust, and your friendship. I wouldn't be doing this without you guys in my life.

Red Rocks Church family: For allowing me to be part of this group of sold out believers living to make heaven more crowded!

Jill: For your love and support that makes everything I do possible.

CONTENTS

Introduction 1

Chapter 1: Crazy Train 5

Chapter 2: Here to There 12

Vehicle 1: Prayer

Chapter 3: The Last Time Prayer Made Sense 23

Chapter 4: What's the Point? 31

Chapter 5: Say What? 44

Vehicle 2: The Bible

Chapter 6: What Now? 57

Chapter 7: What Is This Thing? 62

Chapter 8: What Does It Do? 69

Chapter 9: How Do I Use It? 73

Vehicle 3: Relationships

Chapter 10: Go Live with Your Mom 87

Chapter 11: Why Does This Really Matter? 96

Chapter 12: What Should I Do Now? 106

Vehicle 4: Serving

Chapter 13: A Proud Funeral 117

Chapter 14: Greatness Can Be Bought 127

Chapter 15: McMuffins Change Lives 135

Vehicle 5: Giving

Chapter 16: Show Me the Money 143

Chapter 17: Why Give? 151

Chapter 18: How to Give 155

Vehicle 6: Sharing

Chapter 19: Scared to Death 169

Chapter 20: Lessons at the Well 179

Chapter 21: Worth the Risk 190

Rubber Hits the Road

Chapter 22: The Gas Is on Your Side 195

Chapter 23: Under Caution 201

Chapter 24: Rubber to the Road 209

Notes. 216

INTRODUCTION

Growing up, the idea of God never really made sense to me. I went to church when I had to and bided my time counting ceiling tiles and the minutes until I could leave. If there was a God, I couldn't find any similarities between me and Him and had no idea why the two of us should pretend to be friends. By all accounts, my mom was the only one in our family who seemed to have some connection with Him, and, to be honest, I assumed that her connection was just a crutch to help her get through difficult times.

When I was at church I heard things like: *Jesus loves you, He's the only way to heaven, He wants a life changing relationship with you.*

Unfortunately, I never heard the follow-up on how to make sense of any of those things. *Was God real?* I didn't really know and, to be honest, I didn't have the desire to try to figure it out. *Did He want a life-changing relationship with me?* Probably not. I was nothing like the hand-raising, Bible quoting people I saw in church.

As far as I could tell, getting close to God was all about everything I couldn't do. If I could avoid enough of the bad things, God would be pretty happy with me.

Don't drink, don't smoke, don't chew, and don't date girls who do. Which isn't always an easy task growing up in Kansas!

Being a good Christian seemed to be living a life of refusing to do anything that resembled fun. Stay away from alcohol, drugs, sex, and most forms of dancing, because everyone knows dancing takes you straight to hell. Don't listen to the wrong station on the radio or go to most movies, and whatever you do, don't say, "Dang it!" because apparently that's close enough to a cuss word, and that would fire God right up.

Most of what I knew about God made little to no sense to me, so I just steered clear.

Fast-forward to present day, and people everywhere you look are still asking the same questions.

Is getting close to God really possible? Is it a list of dos and don'ts or a real one-on-one relationship type thing? Does God really change lives today? Will He really change my life?

Whether you are simply curious about God or you've been following Him for most of your life, figuring out how to get closer to Him in a real and authentic way may seem difficult or even impossible at times. That's what *Transit* is all about, getting close to God made simple. God can be everywhere at the same time, which is a mind-blowing concept in and of itself. We're not talking about physically moving closer to God, we're talking about a spiritual journey. This isn't about jumping through hoops, or doing enough good things to capture God's attention or affection. *Transit* is about experiencing the authenticity inside of a relationship with the Creator of the universe. *Transit* is for ordinary, average people like you and me. It's about being able to connect with God in such a real and sensible way that it actually changes our lives on a daily basis.

God has tailor-made some very practical spiritual "vehicles" that are designed to transport us closer and closer in relationship with Him on a consistent basis.

As you turn these pages, we'll begin identifying and putting these "vehicles" into motion. You will quickly learn that you, just the way you are right now, can move into a life altering connection with God. You are about to embark on a journey that's going to change everything about your life. This is a trip you will never forget. I'm excited for you. Enjoy the ride!

Chapter 1

Crazy Train

I stared in the mirror in my bathroom. It was 2:30 a.m., and I could hear Hollywood in the background: sirens, yelling, something breaking, and the faint sound of bass coming from who knows where. I had run into this bathroom, even though the one in my bedroom was closer, because I didn't want the girl in my bed to know I was sick. After all, no one likes a guy who can't handle his drugs.

I'm looking old, I thought, wiping puke from my lips. My eyes were bloodshot and swollen, and my face pale. *How much cocaine did I do? Did I take ecstasy too? What was that last thing she gave me? How'd we even get home?*

The questions came faster than answers as I stumbled through the fog of the past twelve hours of my sorry existence. Tears streamed from my eyes and my hands trembled. The guilt and shame I felt were sickening enough, but the regret I was enduring was overwhelming. Three weeks earlier I had given my life to God and promised Him and myself that this would never happen again, but it did! As I stared at my reflection in the mirror, I realized my ability to commit to things was a joke; and even worse than that, I was a hypocrite.

At that moment my life could be summed up by the lyrics to an old Ozzy Osbourne song:

Mental wounds still screaming
Driving me insane
I'm going off the rails on a crazy train.

For years I had convinced myself that I was living the life. I had graduated from a major university, wedged my foot into the film industry, was meeting famous people, and had easy access to drugs and women. *This was supposed to be the pinnacle of life, right?* I was twenty-four years old and had it all, or so it seemed. I knew it wasn't real. I knew I was living a lie. Life in Hollywood is like a fun house filled with smoke and mirrors. After awhile you don't know what's real and what's not.

"This is what a Christian looks like, huh?" I said with disgust, as I stared at myself in the mirror.

In a useless attempt to make the room stop spinning and to gather my thoughts, I grabbed onto both sides of the sink to steady myself. All I could think about was three weeks earlier when I had gone to church and asked God to forgive me of my sins and for Jesus to be my Savior. That day was surreal. For the first time in my life, I had felt at peace. The burden of my addictions had lifted, and I was convinced the best years of my life were yet to come.

I was positive I would never touch another drug, and I would be a brand-new person from that point on. After all, that's what the church people told me. They said I could live a better life, and I believed them. They told me I would have the power to resist temptation, and I believed them. The biggest promise of all was when they told me I could get close to God and that it would change everything about my life. What they didn't tell me was exactly how to do that. *Maybe they forgot? Maybe they didn't know?* For three long weeks I had held out and tried on my own to be a different person. But since I didn't know how to get close and stay close to God on my own, not only was I throwing away my newfound faith, but I was also about to throw away my entire life in the process.

I wanted to be closer to God. I just didn't know how to get there.

I had great intentions and high hopes for a new life with God. Unfortunately good intentions and hope were not all I needed. I needed to take practical truths from the Word of God and implement them into my life. I needed to take advantage of the very things God promised a long time ago that could bring us into a real and life-changing relationship with Him.

The problem is I didn't know any of these things. I didn't know how to start a relationship with God. I didn't know how to be close to Him. I didn't know what the Bible had to say about any of this, and my lifestyle was about to kill me.

We'll pick my story back up later. For now let's talk about you.

Do you ever wonder if being close to God could really change your life?

Did you ever want to be closer to God but don't really know how to get there?

Do you ever wonder if getting close to God is even possible for someone like you? Or anyone, for that matter?

If so, you're in good company. A lot of people, including me, know your pain.

If you desire to be closer to God today, then this book is for you. Contrary to what you may have experienced or thought before, you can experience God in a real and authentic way. You can be free of addictions. You can have peace, real joy, and a purpose in life. You can live life to the fullest. And you can have these things today!

Regardless of what your past looks like, please know that you can change for the better, but you need God. I know this to be true from firsthand experience. You can experience the life-changing power of God in an undeniable and powerful way. You can move into a closer relationship with Him than you may have ever thought possible. And doing so will change everything about your life. That's not just fancy church talk; its true!

I know because I've experienced it. I've lived it. I've walked through my own personal hell. I know the power of addiction and depression. I'm familiar with suicidal thoughts, and I know the depths of hopelessness and despair. Maybe you do too.

Maybe you know how it feels to be so far from God you can't imagine ever being close to Him. I know what it's like to look around at other Christ followers and think I can never have what they have. I could never be good like they are. I know what it's like to start a relationship with God and have no idea what to do next.

I also know what it's like to follow God for many years, appear to have everything in life perfectly put together, and wake up one day and realize that I'm not as close to God as I pretended to be or wish I were.

But get this: I also know what it's like to experience God in such a real way that it transports you to an entirely different place in life! I know what it's like to go from "here to there." And my hope is that you have that same experience.

Upon giving my life to God, I was promised that I could get close to Him and that it would change my life.

The problem for me was that no one showed me how to get there so I slid back into my old ways. That doesn't have to be your story. The purpose of *Transit* is to show you the modes of transportation that will move you toward God so you don't have to make the same mistakes so many others like me have made.

God's Word gives six specific yet practical ways to get close to Him. These six "vehicles," if you will, are guaranteed to take you closer to God than you are right now. These vehicles are simple to operate and extremely relevant to our lives today. In the pages that follow, you'll be introduced to these vehicles, but more important, you'll learn exactly how to operate each one of them.

The vehicles you'll learn to use are:

1. Prayer
2. The Bible
3. Relationships
4. Serving
5. Giving
6. Sharing

Odds are you've heard and even tried one or more of these six things before. Whether you have or haven't, you're about to embark on a journey where these things will be front-and-center activities that will take you closer to God than you are today.

After finishing this book you'll be able to:

- Talk to God and know exactly why you are doing it and where to start.
- Navigate the Bible, and let God speak to you through it.
- Choose healthy relationships, and know why you're doing it and how it's affecting your future.
- Share what you've experienced, and watch it change you and the lives of your loved ones.
- Make others' lives better by serving them, and experience new-found purpose in life that comes with it.
- Learn why giving of your resources isn't just the right thing to do; it's the thing to do if you want to experience total life change.

This trip you'll be taking toward God will challenge and stretch you, but it will also take you places you've never gone before. This ride will feel like a crazy train of its own at times, but whatever you do, stay put, trust the Driver, and enjoy the ride. Like Corrie ten Boom, a missionary who sacrificed everything so others could know Christ, once said: "When a train goes through a tunnel and it gets dark, you don't throw away the ticket and jump off. You sit still and trust the engineer."

Trust me when I tell you this journey is worth it. So as I said before, sit back, relax (briefly), and enjoy the ride.

Chapter 2

Here to There

I f "here" is where you are today, and "there" is someplace closer to God, where life-change really happens, then get ready because you're on your way from *here* to *there*.

Before we hit the road, I must make something abundantly clear to you. Although we're going to talk about some things you and I can begin to understand and even begin to do, we are *not* earning our salvation. We are *not* going to do anything that will make God love us more. That's not what this is about. My children can't do anything to make me love them more. They have my love, and they'll never have to earn that, but we can do some things that will bring us into a closer relationship as they grow older. My wife Jill and I love each other as much as we are capable of doing. Jill does not have to earn my love today, but every good marriage counselor would tell us we can still do some things that will bring us closer to each other in our relationship. When I refer to "moving closer to God" throughout this book, that's what I mean, our ability to move into a closer, more authentic relationship with God Himself.

God is omnipresent, which means He's everywhere at the same time. So getting closer to Him is not a physical journey; it's a spiritual one. I've met countless people who want an authentic relationship with the Creator of the universe—One who actually has the power to change things in their lives—but they don't even know how to start moving toward such a relationship.

Depending on which polls you read today, about 80 percent of people in the United States claim to believe in God. Whether you fall into that category or not, you've probably heard that Jesus died for your sins, loves you, and wants to have a relationship with you. If that's news to you, He did, He does, and you can!

"For God loved the world in this way: He gave His One and Only Son, so that everyone who believes in Him will not perish but have eternal life" (John 3:16).

God loves you and me so much that He allowed His Son to die an undeserved death on a cross to pay the price for our sins. When you and I put our trust in God, we receive the free gift of eternal salvation. We get to be with God in heaven forever.

In fact, the Bible teaches us that He not only loves us and saves us from our sins, but He wants to be closer than a brother to us here and now.

If you've ever really considered having a close relationship with God, you have to have wondered how in the world that is actually possible. After all, we're talking about a relationship with God. I don't know about you, but I have a hard enough time relating to other messed-up human beings that I can actually see and touch. *A relationship with God?* He's invisible. Perfect. All-knowing. All-powerful. The Creator of the universe. In other words, He's everything I'm not.

Many people I talk to tell me they want to be close to God, if that's really possible, and they want to be in a place where their relationship with God is so real and authentic that it actually impacts their lives. What they're looking for is a destination that has proven elusive for many because they give up too early or don't really know where they're going in the first place. But that elusive place is where a person's life intersects with God's love, grace, and peace. The result is nothing short of phenomenal. That is "there," and that is exactly where we are headed in the following pages.

But let me backtrack to that night in Hollywood when I was on the verge of a drug overdose. The worst part for me about returning to my addiction after giving my life to God was feeling like a failure. Sure, I felt physically ill that night, but the inner turmoil and guilt I was experiencing were far worse than any physical pain I had. And the truth was, I really had tried to be in relationship with God. I really wanted to experience a brand-new life with Him, but after one night of bad decisions, I suddenly convinced myself that getting close to Him in a real and authentic way was just not possible for a person like me. I was too far gone.

Have you tried to get close to God and feel as though you've failed too? Maybe you've been following Christ for a long time and still feel like getting closer to Him is a lot easier to talk about than to do. The truth is, if you're reading this now, you, like most people, know where you want to go. You want to be closer to God; you're just not sure how to get there.

I realize this will not apply to everyone, but if that's you, I'm right there with you. Been there, done that! That night I didn't regret losing something pretend. What I had experienced by committing my life to Christ was real. I had seen that Jesus was more than something—Someone—just to discuss, He is a way of life that brought peace, love, and grace to mine.

After experiencing that, I knew I didn't want some halfhearted, guilt-ridden, fabricated relationship with God, I wanted the real deal. I wanted to talk with and hear from Him. I wanted to know He was there for me at any moment. I wanted to be *there* with Him.

In the years since, I've become convinced of a few things. One of those absolute things is that such a relationship with God is possible. There is a place we really can go with God that changes everything. Listen to what God says about this life-altering location: "'When you come looking for me, you'll find me. 'Yes, when you get serious about finding me and want it more than anything else, I'll make sure you won't be disappointed.' GOD's Decree. 'I'll turn things around for you'" (Jer. 29:13–14 MSG).

Here lies the foundation for us in this great quest to move from here to there. *There* is where God is. And He tells us that where He is, we can find Him.

As I said earlier, the destination we're talking about is not a physical place; it's a spiritual one. God says we can find Him and get to where He is, which means we're not there yet. So there is a spiritual location, and God says when you join Him there, He'll turn your entire life around! When we go from relationally distant from God and move toward real connection with Him, the Bible says it will change everything about our lives today.

That's not just religious talk. It's not make-believe or wishful thinking. I've experienced it. I've come a long way from staring in the mirror so drugged up I could barely stand, questioning God, myself, and life in general, to being a pastor who wants everyone to experience the same real God I have. Let's look at this passage one more time: "'When you come looking for me, you'll find me. Yes, when you get serious about finding me and want it more than anything else, I'll make sure you won't be disappointed.' God's Decree. 'I'll turn things around for you'" (Jer. 29:13–14 MSG).

Isn't that what you really want? Isn't that what you really need?

That's what I needed that night standing in my Hollywood bathroom. I was dealing with a disappointment that night like I had never felt before. What I realize now is I wasn't just disappointed in my actions; I was disappointed that the promise of being close to God, and that my life really mattered, was, in my opinion, a lie. It wasn't attainable, and because it wasn't, I would be stuck with my lot in life for the rest of my days.

I didn't know it at the time, but I didn't have to be stuck in that spot of my life, and the promise of moving closer to God did apply to me. The same holds true for you. If you're not where you want to be in life, you can move forward. You can move from here to there.

The Word of God promises many benefits when we move closer to God and begin to experience His presence and involvement in our lives:

- We will find hope and the future plans God has for us (Jer. 29:11).
- We will experience the best possible life (John 10:10).

- We'll be able to make big decisions and understand God's will for our lives (Acts 2:28).
- We'll finally experience real joy (Acts 2:28).
- We can experience peace in the middle of tragic and/or confusing life events (Phil. 4:7).

King David wrote Psalm 18 about being close to God: "I love you, LORD, my strength. The LORD is my rock, my fortress and my deliverer; my God is my rock, in whom I take refuge, my shield and the horn of my salvation, my stronghold" (Ps. 18:1–2 NIV).

The list goes on and on the more you examine the Bible. Saying that these things will turn our lives around is an understatement. Maybe the best description of the importance of our being transported spiritually can be found in 2 Peter 1:3: "His divine power has given us everything required for life and godliness through the knowledge of Him who called us by His own glory and goodness."

Being there in a close relationship with the Creator of the universe will equip you with every single thing you'll ever need to succeed in this life! Once you really understand the benefits of being closer to God, you will want to go there.

Let me point out one important thing I learned about this journey of moving toward God: I had to make a couple of fundamental decisions. And so will you. I had to decide then, and you'll have to decide now, that not only is this trip worth taking, but you'll be "all in," and you'll stay "all in" for the duration of the ride.

In Texas Hold'em the climax of the card game happens when one player looks another in the eye, pushes all his chips to the middle of the table, and with a Clint Eastwood voice says, "I'm all in." There's no turning back at that point. The player is 100 percent invested in that hand of cards. That's the level of commitment I am asking you to make before you turn the following pages.

If you want to be transported spiritually to a place you can currently only imagine, you're going to have to be "all in." Remember the first verse we looked at in this chapter, "You will seek me and find me when you seek me with all your heart" (Jer. 29:13 NIV). Simply put, God is telling you that you can get there. You can find Him. You can be close to Him. You can experience life-change, but there's one condition: you have to seek Him with all of your heart. You have to be all in!

In the same way we don't want some halfhearted connection with God, He doesn't want halfhearted people seeking Him. Maybe you've tried this before, and you found yourself coming up short of your desired destination. Maybe you didn't really know where you were trying to go in the first place. Maybe, just maybe, you never actually gave God a wholehearted shot. Whatever the reasons may have been in the past, none of that matters now. What matters right now is whether you want to move closer to God. Only you can do this for you.

You now know what the Bible says about being close to God, and now you must decide if you want it. Before you turn the page, before you even get introduced to the first vehicle that will begin taking you closer to God, first take a moment to ask yourself some questions: *Do I really want this? Am I willing to pursue God with all I have?* If you can say yes to both of these questions, then read on!

And remember, you don't have to be perfect. You don't have to have all the answers. You may be completely new to this whole thing. Or you may be a lifelong, battle-scarred Christ follower. It doesn't matter how good or bad life may be going for you right now. It doesn't matter what's happened in your past. This is all about your future. If you're willing to risk trusting God, decide to be all in, and stay all in. You're about to go to a place you have never been before. Hang on because this is a ride you'll never forget.

Vehicle 1

Prayer

Chapter 3

The Last Time Prayer Made Sense

About a month before my drug-induced meltdown, standing in front of the mirror on that crazy night, I got out of bed one morning and assumed the day would be like any other. I rolled a fresh cigarette, stood on my balcony in the heart of Hollywood, California, took in the sun, and got my nicotine fix. Perfect start to another day in paradise, or so I thought. Without warning my mind started taking me to places I'd never been before, and I started thinking about things I'd never considered.

What is the purpose of my life?

If I died tomorrow, would anyone really care?

Do I matter to anyone?

Why am I even alive?

Where did these thoughts come from?!

I wasn't trying to change or be deep or mysterious. In fact, prior to that morning I would have told you I was the happiest man on earth. I lived in Los Angeles, had a job in the film business that I loved, and was dating a girl who had modeling pictures in a store window on Melrose Avenue, which to me, meant I was dating a supermodel. My life was perfect, and now out of nowhere I'm contemplating the meaning of life. It didn't make sense.

Suddenly I realized I didn't know why I was alive. I had no purpose. I wasn't proud of my life, and all I had accomplished of late was getting wasted every night with my friends. While on the balcony that day, I had a moment of clarity, which was really just a moment of realizing I had no clarity.

I dropped the cigarette, not because I was done with it but because I was having an anxiety attack and couldn't breathe. As I gasped for air, I went inside and walked in circles around my apartment trying to catch my breath. Greg, my roommate, walked in and said, "Hey man, you alright?"

I looked at him with tears rolling down my face and said, "I don't think I am."

That was the beginning of the end of my perfect life.

Over the next few days the panic attacks increased, and my ability to control my emotions decreased. I remember calling my mom and saying over and over again, "Mom, I don't know what's wrong with me. I'm losing it."

The panic attacks continued and would surface without warning. I could be driving my car, sitting on the couch, lying in bed, or eating lunch; and the next thing I knew I was scrambling to catch my breath. In the days that followed I stopped eating. Smoking was the only thing that had a calming effect on me. It was a miserable cycle. I knew I needed something; I just didn't really know what that something was. I wanted change, but I didn't know how to get it. I wanted to be in a different place in life; I just didn't know how to get there.

It finally got to a point where I had lost all hope. I sat down at the kitchen table, scattered pills across it, got a big plastic cup of water, and decided enough was enough. A friend of mine had recently attempted suicide with pills, so I knew the recipe. I had the pills, so here we go. With tears running down my face, I decided it was time to clock out. As I reached for the pills, everything began to move in slow motion. I started to feel numb, and my mouth got surprisingly dry. Suddenly a disturbing thought crossed my mind: *Will I go to heaven if I kill myself?*

My mom had given her life to God when I was a kid, and reluctantly I had gone to church with her every now and then. I remember Sunday school teachers talking about heaven and hell, but I couldn't recall exactly what the prerequisites were to get into them, and that scared me. The realization that I wasn't sure where I'd go when I died brought on another anxiety attack.

I can't even kill myself right. I've got to figure this heaven and hell thing out 'cause I'm going to be in one of them in about forty-five minutes. I can't ask my mom; she'll freak out. Maybe I could call Parks. He's a pastor; he'll know what to do.

I dialed Eric Parks. He was my dope-smoking buddy and roommate in college. But during our senior year he found God and left school. Although I didn't understand his newfound faith, we did keep in touch over the years. Parks picked up the phone and sounded surprised that I was calling him, "Johnson?" he said in his upbeat minister-like manner.

I didn't have time for small talk. "Parks, listen, this is kind of crazy, but can you just give me the Cliff's Notes version on heaven and hell?"

"What?" he asked. "What's going on?"

I was so raw and desperate I didn't even care what he thought. I told him what I was doing and asked him to explain the rules on entry to both places. And I asked him again to make it quick.

A lengthy conversation ensued, and miraculously Parks convinced me to put my suicidal plans on hold so I could visit him in Illinois. Since I had planned on being dead that day, my schedule was clear, so I agreed to go. I flew to Rockford, Illinois. I arrived wearing my grey slacks, combat boots, chain-wallet, and thrift-store shirt. Eric picked me up wearing khakis and a freshly ironed, tucked-in Polo button-up. *How were we even friends?* I thought. He was probably thinking the same thing. It had been a few years since we'd seen each other, and he knew I almost killed myself the day before, so the car ride was awkward to say the least. The "How you doing?" "Fine, you?" conversation wasn't really going to cut it on this one. To break the ice I blurted, "I can't believe you're a pastor!"

"I can't believe you almost killed yourself!" He blurted back.

I wasn't sure which one was worse.

We spent the night catching up. I met his wife and baby girl, and then amazingly enough I got a good night's sleep on the couch. The next day he woke me up and said, "Hey, we're going to church."

He brought me out here, so I figured I had to go.

The truth is, I wanted to go. I was curious to see this cult that kidnapped my pot-smoking friend and also secretly hopeful the church experience would be my ticket out of jail. God seemed to have changed Eric's life in dramatic ways, and I needed something similar to happen to me, so *why not?* I changed into another thrift store shirt, checked my wallet for some cocaine for the road, put on my leather jacket, and was ready to roll.

I lit up one last smoke before entering the building, just to make sure everyone there knew I wasn't really joining their club. Eric took me inside, and before I knew it, I was standing in the biggest church room I'd ever seen. People were singing and clapping to a style of music I was not familiar with. And after listening to it for a few minutes, I was glad I was not familiar with it. I did not know people really played tambourines! Everyone was singing about lambs and blood and all kinds of cultish-sounding things. Some of them even raised their hands in the air as if they were signaling a field goal had been kicked. I found a lot of what was happening to be pretty funny. It seemed like a well-oiled circus, and I was sitting way too close to the animals.

Eric sensed my skepticism and took it upon himself to try to explain everything. I could tell he was really embarrassed, and I enjoyed that.

The CEO, the main guy, the "senior pastor," stepped up to the mic behind a podium the size of a small car. Instead of starting his planned sermon, he said something to the effect of: "I was about to start the message, and I just can't. God has put on my heart to pray for someone. I believe someone here needs to experience the life-changing power of God this morning. You need to invite Jesus into your heart. You know who you are, and I believe your life depends on this."

He then invited everyone to come forward to pray. For reasons that didn't make sense to me, my heart started pounding out of my chest, and my eyes flooded with tears. Suddenly, I didn't care how bad the music was or who might be watching me; without thinking, I just started walking to the front. I knelt down and cried like a girl who just got dumped at prom. Parks knelt with me, he put his hand on my shoulder, and he cried too. I didn't know what to do or even what to say. Parks prayed for me, and then he told me to pray. All I knew to say was, "God, I'm sorry." I just kept repeating that over and over.

What a crazy day! I don't know what's more exhausting, contemplating suicide or visiting a church for the first time. After service we went to lunch, and I felt like a new man even though my jacket still reeked of stale cigarette smoke.

"I feel like I just reracked all the weight I was carrying on my shoulders," I told Parks. "I feel light and free. This is weird."

To my surprise and definitely to Parks's surprise, I had somehow become a follower of Christ despite all my opposition. I just decided I was going to put my trust in Him. I asked Him to forgive me of my sins, and according to the Bible I was "saved." I wasn't even sure what it all meant. I just knew I felt better, and Parks assured me I was going to heaven some day. That sounded good enough to me. And it all started with one prayer.

That was the last time, for a long time, I understood what the point of prayer actually was. It made sense that day. I knew what to say: "I'm sorry." And I knew why I was saying it: Because I wanted to go to heaven someday, and I was hoping God would help me out in the meantime. That prayer made sense. Parks told me to start praying every day after that. I remember thinking, *What's the point of praying? And if I did figure that out, what am I supposed to say?*

Has anyone ever told you to pray, or have you ever just felt like you should, started to do so, and thought: *I'm not sure why I'm even doing this. Is anyone really listening? And if I can figure out why I'm attempting this, what am I supposed to say?*

If so, you're not alone. Keep reading. It's time to dig into this.

Chapter 4

What's the Point?

This is where things really start to get good. This is the point where things started to click for me, and they will for you too. Talking to God was the first thing I needed to figure out, and it is for you too.

The first of our six spiritual vehicles is prayer. And as you'll see throughout this section, God promises us that if we'll use this vehicle, it will have life-altering effects on us today, as well as bring us closer to God in the process. Again, you are not going to earn God's love by praying. He already loves you. You are not going to lose your salvation if you don't pray enough or the right way. This is all about how you can move into a closer relationship with God by using this God-given spiritual vehicle. As you would expect, getting closer to anyone involves communication, and the same is true for us and God. Prayer is not a magical language or some mystical action that only certain people can do. Prayer is simply talking with God. The problem for most of us isn't understanding the concept; it's trying to figure out what the point of it is.

Many people today have attempted to take prayer out for a spin once or twice, usually in times of crisis, but most of those same people don't make it a daily practice. And I get it. Prayer can feel awkward because, well, we're talking to Somebody we can't see. My Uncle Bob used to do that, but then again he would also hide behind the curtains and eat pennies. Different story for a different day.

How do we know God's listening? How do we know if we're doing it right? Are people like us allowed to pray about just anything, or are there some rules I don't know about? Do I sit or stand?

Can I open my eyes? It seems standard to close them, and apparently the tighter I close them the better. What about the hand-folding thing, where'd that come from, and is that required?

Take all of the mind games we experience upon attempting to pray, and combine those with the fact that we're really busy, and the last time I prayed it didn't seem to work anyway, and what do you get? A spiritual act that we've all heard of but few of us actually do on a regular basis. *Why?* Because we just don't see the point.

The fact that most of us don't pray on a regular basis isn't even bad news if we don't figure out what the point of prayer actually is. Maybe you're like I was: You've prayed for God to forgive you of your sins, and you've received salvation, which grants us heaven forever. And you've heard you ought to keep on praying, but you're not sure how to take the next step with this spiritual discipline.

What is the point of prayer?

Great question and it deserves a great answer. The Bible shows us many great results in the lives of people who pray. We'll start by looking at the following three reasons we should pray.

1. Prayer changes circumstances.
2. Prayer changes you.
3. Prayer takes you closer to God.

Prayer Changes Circumstances

We pray because it changes things. It brings us peace. It heals. It restores. It provides direction. It puts us in communication with God.

Richard Foster, in his book *Celebration of Discipline*, says: "Real prayer is life creating and life changing. To pray is to change."[1]

Prayer changes things. Jesus prayed often in the mornings (Mark 1:35). His disciples prayed consistently (Acts 6:4), and if we want to experience life-change and a newfound closeness to God, we'll need to learn to do the same.

The Word of God reiterates this over and over again. When lives were on the line, when the future depends on it, when people are hungry, thirsty, sick, even dying, God proves time and time again that He will change things when people pray.

From the Bible we see God parting rivers and seas because people prayed. When the Israelites were wandering around the desert, God dropped food out of the sky because somebody prayed. God calmed storms on the sea and gave water from a rock because somebody prayed. God saved men from a burning furnace; He gave a ninety-year-old woman the gift of pregnancy because people prayed. He healed the blind, cured diseases, and raised the dead because people prayed. The message God is giving us from His Word is loud and clear: when people pray, God intervenes. When people pray, things change!

"Jesus Christ is the same yesterday, today, and forever" (Heb. 13:8).

That means if He changes things for people who prayed in Bible times, He'll change things for people who pray today. And as you can see from His résumé, He's into changing big things in big ways. He can help us overcome depression and addictions. He can mend relationships we thought were too far gone. He can heal sickness. He can provide financially to meet our needs. He can restore broken and wounded hearts. But we have to pray.

As Bill Hybels said in the best book on prayer I've ever read, *Too Busy Not to Pray*, "Prayer-less people cut themselves off from God's prevailing power, and the frequent result is the familiar feeling of being overwhelmed, overrun, beaten down, pushed around, defeated. Surprising numbers of people are willing to settle for lives like that. Don't be one of them. Nobody has to live like that. Prayer is the key to unlocking God's prevailing power in your life."[2]

God is no respecter of persons, and He loves to do the impossible. So start praying and give Him the opportunity to amaze you! For some people simply being reminded of how God's power shows up when we pray is enough, but for some of us stubborn kids, we still have more questions.

Have you ever thought that if God was all-knowing then He already knows what you and I need, so praying is still sort of a waste of time? Or did I just bring up a question you've never asked, but now you must know the answer, and you want to pray less now than you did twenty seconds ago? Sorry about that. People struggle with that question all the time, as I did, until I actually read about this topic in the Bible. God is clear that it doesn't work that way. He wants us to talk to Him about our battles and to engage Him in the issues we are facing. He wants us to pray, and then, He says, He will unleash His power into our lives.

We see a great example of this in Exodus 17:10–13. A guy named Joshua was in a battle, a battle God wanted him to win. Moses was watching this battle from a hill above. Moses was holding his hands up in the air and praying for Joshua and his troops while they were fighting. Watch what happened:

> Joshua did as Moses had told him, and fought against Amalek, while Moses, Aaron, and Hur went up to the top of the hill. While Moses held up his hand, Israel prevailed, but whenever he put his hand down, Amalek prevailed. When Moses' hands grew heavy, they took a stone and put it under him, and he sat down on it. Then Aaron and Hur supported his hands, one on one side and one on the other so that his hands remained steady until the sun went down. So Joshua defeated Amalek and his army with the sword.

When Moses prayed, they won. When Moses quit praying, they lost. God knew what they needed the whole time. God wanted to intervene the whole time. God wanted to change things for them the whole time. But God's power was only unleashed when prayer was happening. And the same holds true for you and me today. It's not enough for us to assume God knows what we need and He'll take care of it. God says, "If you want Me to change things, then I want you to talk to Me about it first." When we refuse to talk to God about our situations in life, we tie God's hands from intervening in our lives.

John Wesley, an esteemed theologian, put it like this, "God does nothing but in answer to prayer."

When we're idle, God is idle. But when we hop into the driver's seat of this spiritual vehicle and actually take it out onto the road, it changes everything. When you and I stop and talk to God about the things going on in our lives, that's when He gets involved. That's when His power shows up, and that's when things start to change. We pray because it changes things.

Prayer Changes You

The second reason to pray is because it changes you. This is huge and so many people miss it! So often you and I gauge the effectiveness of our prayers by whether we got what we wanted, right? I prayed that my Aunt Jane would not die of cancer, but she died. Nothing happened as the result of my consistently begging God to heal her, except that I got really angry and confused with God. Then I convinced myself that prayer didn't really do anything. From that moment on I was paralyzed by the question, "What is the point of prayer?"

Have you experienced the same thing in your own life? You really wanted something, and you broke down and asked God to do it. In fact, you begged God to do it, and He didn't. Not only were you mad at, hurt by, and disappointed in God, but you also convinced yourself that prayer doesn't really do that much.

Even when we don't feel it and can't see it, prayer always works, every single time, but we don't always get what we want. Let me say that again: Prayer always works, but we don't always get what we want.

Those two things must be separated in our minds, and for some of you, this is the first time you've ever thought about prayer like this. God won't always say yes, but prayer still works. That's a tough concept to understand.

God refers to Himself as an all-knowing, all-loving Father. If you are a parent, you know all too well that you can't always say yes to your kids, regardless of how much you love them. In fact, because you love them, you say no from time to time.

My four-year-old son recently asked me if he could go play in the street in front of our house. I told him that Mommy and I couldn't come outside at the moment so the answer was no. His body immediately went limp; he dropped to the floor in what appeared to be some sort of convulsion and began throwing the craziest temper tantrum I've ever seen. He was screaming and kicking. He even took a swing at a pair of shoes on the floor next to him. I remember thinking, *I think I'm supposed to discipline him for stuff like this,* but I couldn't stop laughing so I walked away and asked Jill to deal with it. She was superhappy with me.

As a loving father who just understands things my kids don't, there are times when I can't say yes to their wishes regardless of how much I love them. The same holds true for God, our heavenly Father, as it pertains to us His children. Scripture says: "'For as the sky soars high above earth, so the way I work surpasses the way you work, and the way I think is beyond the way you think'" (Isa. 55:9 MSG).

This means that there are times when we ask God for something, in fact beg Him for something, and He won't do what we are sure He should do, and we'll have no clue why. We won't understand why He didn't do what we asked for, because He thinks beyond the way we think. I've been there. We may even drop to the floor and throw temper tantrums from time to time. I've been there too. I've prayed for people to be healed, and I've clearly explained to God why He should do what I think is best, and then when He didn't do it, I was appalled. I was angry, hurt, and confused. I get it. You get it; you've been there too. You, too, have probably been let down when God didn't act according to your wishes in the past. There are times when for reasons we'll never understand until we see God in heaven that He just won't always do what we ask.

But you have to get this: that doesn't mean prayer didn't work. That doesn't mean God is not active and working in your life. It doesn't mean His life-changing power is not in motion. It appears that way to us at times, but it's not the case. I said it earlier: every time we pray, it works!

The apostle Paul was trying to explain this same concept to a church he had started in a city known as Philippi: "Don't worry about anything, but in everything, through prayer and petition with thanksgiving, let your requests be made known to God. And the peace of God, which surpasses every thought, will guard your hearts and minds in Christ Jesus" (Phil. 4:6–7).

Paul advises us to pray about everything, and when we do, we are guaranteed that God's peace will protect our hearts and our minds. We are not guaranteed a yes to everything we pray for. But God's peace is guaranteed every time we pray. God's grace and mercy are also guaranteed every time we pray. "Therefore let us approach the throne of grace with boldness, so that we may receive mercy and find grace to help us at the proper time" (Heb. 4:16).

I imagine God saying it like this, "When you come to Me in prayer, I will enter your life and your situation, and I will give you the strength and ability, comfort and support you need so you can experience peace in such a miraculous way that it won't even make sense!" I picture Him pulling us closer so we can feel His presence and continue: "I may not change your situation exactly the way you would like in the time frame you would like, but every time you pray, I will change you! Because of My grace and mercy and the peace I will enable you to experience, you will make it through this. You will overcome. You will be victorious because My life-changing power is active in your life every time you talk to Me."

A yes from God will change one circumstance in your life, but His mercy, grace, and peace will change everything about every circumstance from here to eternity. We receive God's grace, mercy, and peace *every* time we pray, and that will *change us*.

It's hard for us to understand this, especially in difficult times; but more than getting a yes from God, what we really want is God. A yes changes a few things about our lives; God's grace, mercy, and peace change our entire life. You pray because it changes you.

Had I been able to access God's grace, mercy, and authentic peace, I wouldn't have been running back to narcotics for comfort. I wouldn't have been looking for approval through women. I was a good person craving good things; I just didn't know where to find them. What I didn't realize is that the peace I was dying to feel was available to me through simply talking with God. What I didn't realize is that prayer would change me.

Prayer Takes You Closer to God

We pray because it will bring us closer to God, and that's the point of this journey.

Dallas Willard, philosopher and author, writes, "In addition to all other work that gets done through prayer, perhaps the greatest work of all is the knitting of the human heart together with the heart of God."

Paul said something similar thousands of years earlier when he proclaimed that God would guard our hearts and minds (see Phil. 4:7).

We just looked at this passage: "Don't worry about anything, but in everything, through prayer and petition with thanksgiving, let your requests be made known to God. And the peace of God, which surpasses every thought, will guard your hearts and minds in Christ Jesus" (Phil. 4:6–7).

Ask any member of the Secret Service, and he or she will tell you that you can't guard somebody from across town. You have to be right there with them to shield them from attacks. You have to be up close and personal. What Paul was telling the church in Philippi, and what God is telling us today, is that a by-product of talking to God is being close to Him. As with any relationship you are trying to improve (attention husbands), the more we talk, the closer we get.

God says, "Pray and I'll be right there with you, protecting you, empowering you, and changing you. I won't watch you fight the battle, I'll fight it with you, and when you can do no more, I'll fight it for you." And that's exactly how God's power collides with our lives every time we pray.

Simply put, moving closer to God won't happen for you and it won't happen for me until the prayer vehicle is put into motion.

Chapter 5

Say What?

E ven after we wrap our minds around some of the reasons to start praying, we still have to figure out how to do it. Have you ever sat down to pray and felt like a ninth-grade boy, asking his date to the prom? *I'd really like to say something meaningful here, I just have no idea where to begin, and could you look into my eyes and not at that zit on my cheek.*

Prayer has many great features, and understanding some of them will hopefully get you excited about taking this vehicle out on the road. But to do that you'll need not only to appreciate what it can do but be able to operate it as well.

How Do I Pray? Where Do I Start? What Should I Say?

When I first became a Christ follower, Parks told me I should start praying every day. I wasn't completely comfortable with the idea, but he was a pastor so I figured I'd better listen. I tried. I would sit by myself for an hour every morning "talking to God." At least that's what I'd tell people I was doing. But more times than not, I stared at the ceiling for an hour or so in the mornings thinking about girls, what the day held, and where I was going to lunch. I was single and pretty sure God understood. But it was frustrating for me. I understood and appreciated the value of talking to God, but when I actually tried to do it, I felt inept, awkward, unprepared, unworthy, and confused. After all, God is God and I'm just me.

If you've ever felt even remotely the same way, have no fear. You are not alone. Jesus' disciples had some of the same questions about prayer that we have today: "He was praying in a certain place, and when He finished, one of His disciples said to Him, 'Lord, teach us to pray, just as John also taught his disciples'" (Luke 11:1).

This is a request from someone who was hanging out with Jesus in the flesh on a daily basis! This should make us all feel better. These guys walked and talked with Jesus. They ate with Him and hung out with Him. These guys actually heard Jesus pray multiple times, and they still weren't sure how to start doing it for themselves. After summoning the courage to ask Him how to pray, Jesus said this in response:

Therefore, you should pray like this:

Our Father in heaven,
Your name be honored as holy.
Your kingdom come.
Your will be done
on earth as it is in heaven.
Give us today our daily bread.
And forgive us our debts,
as we also have forgiven our debtors.
And do not bring us into temptation,
but deliver us from the evil one.
[For Yours is the kingdom and the power
and the glory forever. Amen.] (Matt. 6:9–13)

Jesus is telling His disciples, and us today, that we can talk to God anytime. No reservations needed. No need to jump through crazy hoops. No talk of eyes open or closed, hands folded or open—just simple instruction on conversation with the Father. And if you notice, Jesus brings up five distinct conversational topics for His friends and for us to start talking to God about as we begin praying.

He says start by praising and thanking God. He then encourages them to repent of past sins and to ask for things they need. He tells them to ask God to make His will happen in their lives and to show them where to go and where not to go in the future. These five conversation pieces make for a great starting place for you and me to begin talking with confidence to God today.

I can barely remember what I have for lunch each day so I needed to figure out a way of remembering these five topics in my daily prayers. I came up with this acrostic: PRAYS.

Thinking about the word PRAYS helps me remember each of the five topics I want to cover in daily prayer. And if you're feeling a lack of structure in your prayer life, the word PRAYS will help you get this vehicle off and running in no time. It goes like this:

Praise
Repent
Ask
Your Will
Show Me

Say this out loud a few times before you move on. Really—say it out loud three times before you keep reading.

Often when I'm going to pray, I remember what each letter stands for, I talk to God about each one of those things in order, and I know if nothing else, I'm talking to God about the things Jesus instructed. And you can do the same thing:

Praise

"Therefore, you should pray like this: Our Father in heaven, Your name be honored as holy." (Matt. 6:9)

By Jesus telling us to begin prayer time with praises, He is just repeating what the writer of Psalm 100 said hundreds of years earlier about prayer: "Enter His gates with thanksgiving and His courts with praise. Give thanks to Him and praise His name" (Ps. 100:4).

We should start our time in prayer by praising and thanking God for all He has done for us. Here's how I begin my prayers: "God You're so great. You're loving, forgiving, and patient. You've blessed me with so much. Thank You for my family, my friends, my house, car, job, everything."

You get the idea. If you're like me, if you don't purposefully begin with praising and thanking God, most of our prayer times are simply complaining sessions and wish lists we've created for God to fulfill. Jesus says there is a time and place for wishes and complaints, but don't make that your only topic of conversation. Start out by simply praising and thanking your God.

Repent

"And forgive us our debts, as we also have forgiven our debtors." (Matt. 6:12)

My kids don't usually want to talk to me when they think I'm mad. And when it comes to God, I know how my kids feel. When I've sinned or have not lived up to the benchmarks God has set for me, I don't feel worthy to talk to Him, so oftentimes, when I'm feeling guilty, I just don't. Repenting releases me from those feelings, helps me get things straight with God, so I can move onto talking to Him about what's next in life.

> If we confess our sins, He is faithful and righteous to forgive us our sins and to cleanse us from all unrighteousness. (1 John 1:9)

We may not always feel forgiven immediately upon repenting, but the truth of the Word of God trumps our feelings. When we repent, we are forgiven—not because we deserve it but because Jesus died and covered our sins on the cross thousands of years ago. That means we become perfect and "righteous" in God's sight. The moment we honestly seek repentance, we have assurance that we are perfect in our Father's eyes, and that should free us to talk openly and honestly with Him.

Ask

> "Give us today our daily bread." (Matt. 6:11)

After we spend time praising and thanking God, then repenting of our sins, we have every right to come to our Father and ask for things we want and/or need. Nothing is too big, and nothing is too small for us to bring to God. He wants to hear it all. He's not a judge with His arms folded in the sky; He's your heavenly Father who can't wait to hear your requests.

Your Will

> "Your kingdom come. Your will be done on earth as
> it is in heaven." (Matt. 6:10)

Jesus said after you present your requests to God, always follow that up with "Your will be done."

When you actually start praying this way, here's what you are saying to God, "I know what I really want to happen, but I ultimately put my trust in You."

We don't know it and usually can't see it, but what we want in our lives—way more than what we want—is what He wants for our lives! And so we muster up the courage to say, "Not my will but Your will be done."

Jesus didn't just tell us to pray this way; He modeled it for us. You may remember the night He was arrested and taken later to be beaten within an inch of His life and hung on a cross to die. He prayed to the Father. His life was on the line. His prayers were, like ours at times, life and death.

> Then Jesus came with them to a place called
> Gethsemane, and He told the disciples, "Sit here while
> I go over there and pray." Taking along Peter and the
> two sons of Zebedee, He began to be sorrowful and

deeply distressed. Then He said to them, "My soul is swallowed up in sorrow—to the point of death. Remain here and stay awake with Me." Going a little farther, He fell facedown and prayed, "My Father! If it is possible, let this cup pass from Me. Yet not as I will, but as You will." (Matt. 26:36–39)

You want to grow up spiritually? You want to go somewhere you've never been before? You want to experience a closeness to God that you've only heard others talk about? Have the courage not to try to control God with your prayers, but actually let Him control you through your prayers. To get from here to there, start talking to God like this: "God, with every ounce of my being, this is what I want You to do, but I trust You more than I trust me, so not my will, but Your will be done." Few people have the guts to pray this way, but those who do are transported spiritually to a place few people ever see.

Show Me

"And do not bring us into temptation, but deliver us from the evil one." (Matt. 6:13)

We finish up our prayer time with something like this: "God, show me where to go and what to do. Show me where not to go and what not to do." This type of prayer will change the direction of your life forever.

The Lord will always lead you. (Isa. 58:11)

God wants to lead you through this life. He wants to
help you make big decisions and little decisions. He wants
to communicate with you about real things in your life
today, and He'll begin doing this as you pray these kinds of
prayers. You want to know whom to marry, where to live,
which job to take, what investments to make. We have real
questions and real issues, and God wants to get involved in
a real way. He says it starts with us asking Him to show us.

Now if any of you lacks wisdom, he should ask God,
who gives to all generously and without criticizing,
and it will be given to him. (James 1:5)

PRAYS
Praise
Repent
Ask
Your Will
Show Me

I've talked to people who are just beginning conversations with God, and I've talked to people who have been
praying their entire lives, who claim that this tool for talking
to God has changed their prayer life, changed their connection with God, and brought them into a more intimate

relationship with Him than they've ever had before. It will do the same thing for you today.

Spend some time talking to God about each of these topics, and before you know it, you've been talking to God about some life-altering things. In fact, you'll probably run out of time before you run out of things to say. God is your heavenly Father, so you can talk to Him about anything and everything, but if you're at a loss for words, this acrostic will help you get your vehicle out of the driveway and onto the road.

Let me wrap this topic up by making one last observation about Jesus' instructions to us about prayer. It's supposed to happen daily!

"Give us today our daily bread" (Matt. 6:11). Prayer is a daily driver!

For me, starting a relationship with God felt like I had just been thrown a rope as I dangled from the side of a cliff. My newfound faith had saved my life, but I was still holding on for dear life. I needed to continue holding on. I couldn't hold on one day, then let go for a few days. I'd never make it. I had to hold on every single day and day-by-day, inch-by-inch, move my hands toward the top of the rope toward God, toward the life I really wanted. I learned early on that if I wanted to pursue God, prayer had to be daily.

My communication with Him had to become job one for me, and the same thing holds true for you today. Think about it this way: Jesus' disciples, the heroes of our faith, the guys who started the church, were told they had to hold on to prayer every single day if they were going to make it. Jesus told His disciples this vehicle is to be driven "each day," and He's telling us the same thing today.

Collectors of rare cars often have daily drivers and Sunday strollers. Daily drivers get used all the time, but Sunday strollers are so nice that they only come out of the garage on special occasions and sunny Sunday afternoons. Unfortunately many people today treat prayer like those Sunday strollers. It only gets used on the weekends for church and on rare occasions in times of desperation. Simply put, that's not good enough when it comes to prayer, not if you want to get top performance out of this vehicle. God gave us prayer to use on a daily basis.

If you're like me, that means scheduling a time to talk to God ahead of time. Put it on your calendar, plug it into your phone, and tell your assistant, your spouse, or a friend. Ask them to remind you of your commitment to pray and to hold you accountable. Prayer is one of those things nobody else can do for you. You have to choose to do this for yourself.

Prayer is a spiritual vehicle that will take you closer to God as soon as you begin to use it. This journey isn't about wishful thinking or good intentions so get going on this one today! You can do this, and you're going to be so thankful that you did!

Vehicle 2

The Bible

Chapter 6

What Now?

Well-meaning church members had all kinds of advice
for me in the days after I committed my life to Christ.
As the newly saved druggie, I was a favorite "project"
for many of them, and although I didn't crave the attention,
I was appreciative of their concern for my spiritual well-
being. Countless times my new friends told me to pray and
read the Bible.

I didn't own a Bible, and I didn't know there were stores
that sold such a book, but I always nodded confidently and
said, "Oh yeah, of course I'll read the Bible."

This may have been some of the best acting I'd ever
done because, truth be told, I had no idea how to even begin
reading the Bible. That may sound strange to some, but
I am absolutely serious about this. I had no clue what the
Bible really was, what it could do, or how I could use it.

As my time with Parks in Rockford was coming to an end, I began to feel nervous. As much as I wanted to stay in the cozy confines of the Christian community where I had found Christ, it was time to leave, get back to the real world, and maybe even test my newfound faith. After all, I had a lot of cleaning up to do back in Los Angeles. I needed to explain to my producer why I left without warning and in the middle of filming. I needed to face my friends and tell them that I believed in Jesus, and I needed to see if my faith was real. None of this sounded fun.

Just before I left Rockford, Parks baptized me in a lake. I wasn't really sure what that meant either, but it all felt so good, I just went with it. But as soon as I came up from the water, I asked myself, "Now what?"

As I left to go back to Hollywood, where God is not on most people's radar, I was assured I could seamlessly get back to my life in L.A. and continue growing closer to God. My new Illinois Christian friends gave me the ole "Go get 'em kid" pat on the back and sent me on my way with tons of encouragement and prayers. I doubted it would be as easy as they said, but I smiled and said, "Thanks," and hopped my flight to go home.

Within hours of arriving in L.A., I was right back in the swing of things. I went to see some friends and realized my L.A. life was exactly as I'd left it. My buddies were doing what they normally did: drinking alcohol, smoking joints, and snorting cocaine. Everything was back to normal except for me.

I wasn't drinking, smoking, or snorting anymore, and my sudden change had all my buddies wondering what was up. I sensed they knew something was different, but nobody inquired, which was good because I didn't have a clue what I'd say about my new faith.

My time in Rockford would not resonate with my friends in Hollywood. These guys wore wife beaters and combat boots, carried chain wallets, and had lip rings and tattoos. Parks had told me I had become a new creation in Christ and it didn't matter what I wore, but I certainly couldn't see myself explaining this to my L.A. friends. So, for three painful weeks, I tried my best to live up to my new faith by not drinking, not doing drugs, not going out, and not sleeping with girls I met in clubs. The only vice I couldn't forgo was my cigarettes, so I kept smoking.

As I negotiated awkward social situations and dodged any conversation that might reveal what had really happened while I was away, I kept thinking over and over, *What now? What am I supposed to do now?*

Maybe you know that feeling? Maybe you were baptized, and right about the time you dried off and headed back to the real world, you too thought, *What am I supposed to do now?* Or maybe you raised your hand at a church when the preacher asked who wanted to receive Christ as their

Savior and it felt good, but the moment you hit the parking lot, you too were asking the same question. Countless people told me to read my Bible. Not knowing any better, I enthusiastically embraced the idea. With great determination I went to a coffee shop on Melrose Avenue, in the heart of the Hollywood scene, sat at a metal table on the sidewalk and coolly placed my lighter and cigarettes next to my shiny new Bible.

With great flair I opened my Bible and pressed the cover back to crease it. Immediately, my eyes were drawn to the table of contents and a list of strange words.

Genesis
Exodus
Leviticus
Numbers
Deuteronomy

"Ugh!" I said as my eyes ran down the list, "I didn't get the English version!"

Just before I gave up, I saw some familiar names: Matthew, Mark, Luke, John. I had no idea those were books in the Bible, but at least they gave me a rough baseline to get started.

As I stared at the table of contents, I decided I'd read about Matthew. He sounded fairly normal. I looked for corresponding page numbers and then suddenly worried that I might be breaking some unwritten rule by not starting at the beginning. Fearful that a veteran reader might happen to be seated near me, I looked around to find anyone who might have Bible etiquette. I didn't see anyone I deemed to be particularly focused enough on spiritual things, but I did notice that a famous movie star was sitting across from me. From what I could overhear by eavesdropping on their conversation, he was concerned about not having enough furniture, and should he have a place in L.A. and New York. His friend nodded at whatever he said. With little restraint or remorse, I kept listening to their conversation. Every word he said seemed so intriguing; he was what I moved to L.A. hoping to become.

No! No! Focus on your Bible!

Since I had no clue how to start reading my Bible, I lit up another smoke and just stared at it as if I'd stumbled across a small alien life force. Sure, I really wanted to do the Christian thing and get close to God, and if my friends in Rockford were right, reading the Bible was the way to do it. But I didn't have a clue how to move past the table of contents. I needed someone to give me a five-minute lesson on what the Bible was, what it did, and how I could use it.

I just needed a brief introduction to this thing that so many Christians had promised would be life-transforming. Unfortunately for me, I didn't know anyone in Hollywood who could help me out in this capacity, so I finished my smoke, packed up my stuff, and left.

Chapter 7

What Is This Thing?

I suppose, at that time in my life, handing me a Bible was similar to handing an infant an iPhone. I had no experience, training, or any idea how to handle something so powerful, so far-reaching, and so transformative.

What I needed to know then, and what you need to know today, is that the Bible is a gift from God to us, and if we allow it, the Bible can transport us not only toward a better life but also into a stronger relationship with Him. Let me unpack what the Bible is so you will have a better understanding of what it can do for you and how you can use it in order to have a closer relationship with God.

Greg Hawkins and Cally Parkinson wrote a book titled *Move*. They surveyed a thousand church leaders and more than 250,000 congregants, and found that "nothing has more spiritual impact than reflection on scripture."[3]

I think Jesus would agree with their assessment. He said the Bible is to one's spirit what food is to one's body: it's absolutely essential to sustain life. In Matthew 4:4, He put it like this: "Man must not live on bread alone but on every word that comes from the mouth of God."

To help put some guardrails on what the Bible is, realize first that it's not just a book, even though for simplicity's sake I'll call it a book throughout *Transit*. The Bible is actually a collection of books that has held up to centuries of scrutiny from scholars and scientists alike. In fact, the Bible has not taken only its barbs and jabs; it has flourished under the pressure. Here are some impressive facts and achievements to consider:

- The Bible has been translated into more than twelve hundred languages, making it the most translated book of all time.
- The Bible is the best-selling book of all time.
- The main theme of the Bible is God's love for His people and His plan to restore their lives.
- The Bible was written over a period of about fifteen hundred years, by forty plus authors on three different continents.
- The Bible is full of facts, eyewitness accounts, parables, miracles, lessons, and stories, but there is not one contradiction in it.

Stop and reread that last point, and try to imagine the time, the people, the congruency, and the impossibility of mere humans trying to assimilate such a piece of literature.

The next thing you need to understand is that the Bible is trustworthy.

This is big because we live in a Wikipedia world where anyone can post anything, anytime, and pretend it's true. Because of this, skepticism runs rampant, and the truth is not always what it seems; but when it comes to the Bible, its veracity checks out every time.

Without a doubt the Bible is historically accurate. And that's not just good-intentioned church talk. Every archeological finding known to humankind has eventually backed up the Bible's accuracy and authenticity. Out of all the historians, all the archeologists, and every single historical artifact ever discovered and studied, not one of them has ever disproven one line of the Bible! Jewish archeological expert Nelson Glueck sums it up like this: "It may be categorically stated that no archaeological discovery has ever controverted a biblical reference."

That's crazy evidence for the accuracy of the Bible. Knowing it is "spot on" historically should be huge in your faith because when you begin reading about the life of Jesus Christ you can feel assured that what you're reading is not creative invention or wishful thinking, but rather 100 percent historically accurate. Look at Matthew, Mark, Luke, and John. These books give four eyewitness accounts of the life of Jesus; today they are known as the Gospels.

These four books are filled with firsthand accounts of Jesus' life and were used widely in the first-century church to promote the good news of Jesus Christ. If these accounts were falsified in any way, the people during that time, especially Jesus' detractors, would have refuted every point, but they didn't! They couldn't! Those individuals accepted the life, death, and resurrection of Jesus Christ as fact because of the overwhelming eyewitness testimonies given to them in the books of Matthew, Mark, Luke, and John.

Those that lived in and around Jerusalem when Jesus walked the earth could have been the greatest skeptics ever to have lived. But they weren't. *Why?* Because they had firsthand knowledge of when Jesus was killed and when He came back to life. Not only did many of them not refute the accounts of these events, but they put their faith in Him and what the Gospels professed. So many could have claimed the Gospels and the eyewitnesses were crazy, but they didn't! Instead. Even the naturally skeptical helped promote these books. In due time the life, death, and resurrection of Jesus spread around the world because of it's undeniable, irrevocable, factual evidence.

Here's a really cool thing to keep in mind as you contemplate the veracity of the Bible. While leaders of other world religions say things like, "God told me this," or, "An angel told me that," there isn't a single shred of evidence to prove their claims. Just the statement, "Just trust me; it's true." This is not the case with the Bible. It is based on historical events that can be proved with physical evidence! Isn't that awesome? Let that build your faith today. For skeptics of Jesus, proof can be found in actual events in history, physical evidence, eyewitness testimony, and archeological findings. The Bible has more physical evidence proving its accuracy and authenticity than any ancient writing known to man! Because of that you can read this amazing "book" with 100 percent confidence that what you're reading is true.

You should also know that the Bible is God talking directly to us.

Knowing this would have made such a huge difference for me. When I returned to Hollywood, I had no idea God actually communicated to His followers through the Bible.

Back when I first became a Christ follower, the writers of the Bible seemed to be nothing more than well-meaning people who wrote down cool stories and probably made a few up along the way. And while I was sure it was interesting reading, if you're into that sort of thing, how much could guys wearing robes and Birkenstocks really have in common with me? I was so wrong. Since then, I've realized that the Bible is God's inspired words perfectly written to be relevant to you and to me whatever our past, present, or future may be.

Perhaps you've never thought about the Bible as being inspired by God and written just for you, but it's true. Sounds crazy, right?

God makes clear that every single word in the Bible is directly from Him. We find proof of this in Exodus 24:4, "Moses wrote down all the words of the LORD." In 2 Samuel 23:2, this is reinforced, "The Spirit of the LORD spoke through me, His word was on my tongue." In Jeremiah 26:2, the prophet writes, "This is what the LORD says: Stand in the courtyard of the Lord's temple and speak all the words I have commanded you to speak to all Judah's cities that are coming to worship there. Do not hold back a word."

The books known as Judges, Samuel, Isaiah, Haggai, and Zechariah all start with: "This is what the LORD says." The point not to miss here is that the authors are bringing attention to the fact that the words within the Bible are not man's words; they're God's words.

The apostle Paul sums it all up in 2 Timothy 3:16–17, "All Scripture is inspired by God and is profitable for teaching, for rebuking, for correcting, for training in righteousness, so that the man of God may be complete, equipped for every good work."

Admittedly, I was clueless to all these truths as I sat in that café listening to famous people talk about their lives. Maybe you are too! Regardless of your past knowledge and experience of the Word of God, you need to know that the Bible's present value for your life can't be emphasized enough.

The Bible isn't just a book; it's a historically perfect account of the history of God and His Son. It is the primary way God will speak to you as you find your spiritual footing and even for the rest of your life. So don't fall into the trap of not using the Bible to get close to God; it's nothing but a dead end.

Chapter 8

What Does It Do?

Now that you know what the Bible is, you need to know what it can do. The simple answer is: everything!

These two passages are reminders that the Bible allows us to tap into the power of God, to do every good work that God has planned for us: "All Scripture is inspired by God and is profitable for teaching, for rebuking, for correcting, for training in righteousness, so that the man of God may be complete, equipped for every good work" (2 Tim. 3:16–17). "For the word of God is living and powerful" (Heb. 4:12 NKJV).

Sounds impossible, right? You and I can tap into the Creator of the universe's power grid? No matter how insane that sounds, it's true!

Through the Bible, you can access the power of God to:

- Overcome fear and anxiety.
- Conquer depression and persevere through tragedy.

- Pursue your dreams in the way God has created you to do.
- And much, much more.

Think of it this way: if you need wisdom, strength, insight, courage, power, or grace, you need God to help you. All of those things and more can be found in the Bible. It will become your secret source for success! "This book of instruction must not depart from your mouth; you are to recite it day and night so that you may carefully observe everything written in it. For then you will prosper and succeed in whatever you do" (Josh. 1:8).

As you move into a deeper relationship with God, you are going to notice that He will change your priorities and give you dreams and desires you may have never had. Part of fulfilling those dreams and desires the way God wants you to will require spending time in His Word, exploring all the possibilities. "Your word is a lamp for my feet and a light on my path" (Ps. 119:105).

Spending time reading and studying the Bible is like holding a lamp over your path on a dark night. Think of the difference if you were out hiking an unfamiliar trail at night with and without a flashlight. In one scenario your flashlight guides you safely past the exposed roots, rocks, holes, and low-hanging branches. In the second scenario you wouldn't be able to see any of those things. To say the least, you would have a long night in front of you. The

Bible is your flashlight for navigating life. It will show you exactly where the next step should be, and it'll keep you from twisting an ankle, poking your eye out, or walking off the edge of a cliff. Everyone needs this tool—especially when life confronts you with challenges, opportunities, and decisions.

Should I go to college? It's a great job offer, but should I move to another state? Could I really spend the rest of my life with her? What about our dream house that's just outside the school district our kids are thriving in? Do I buy or sell? Do I start that? Stop this? Where do I go from here? Whom do I go with?

All of us have big decisions to make. Those decisions have the power to impact the rest of our lives. God says the Bible will guide us through them, pointing us toward our dreams and helping us to succeed.

All the vehicles explored in *Transit*, including the Bible, move us closer to God. We're reminded of the transporting possibilities of the Word of God in Proverbs 4:20–22: "My son, pay attention to my words; listen closely to my sayings. Don't lose sight of them; keep them within your heart. For they are life to those who find them, and health to one's whole body."

Notice the verse starts out with the reference to a "son." This is God's way of showing you that time spent in His Word is all about relationship with Him. And He doesn't have an at-arm's-length relationship in mind. Instead, the relationship He wants is between a loving Father and a prized child. Talk about life-changing movement!

Chapter 9

How Do I Use It?

Knowing what the Bible is and what it can do for us is meaningless unless we also know how to navigate through it. For many people the Bible can be like the cockpit of an airplane with all of its buttons, levers, lights, dials, and gauges. Most people have seen the inside of a cockpit, but few could actually operate the plane. The Bible can be just as daunting with its Old and New Testaments, Gospels, Epistles, and Prophets. Getting the most out of the Bible without some sort of special training can feel as awkward as flying a plane without having any lessons. Many people today feel that flying solo with the Word of God should be reserved for experts. You know, only pastors, theologians, and those who have been highly trained to operate all those confusing switches.

Don't believe that for a second! The Bible is loaded with promises, wisdom, grace, and peace. That's good news. The better news is that all of that and more are accessible to everyone! So don't assume, like I did at the café in L.A., that you can't figure out how to use the Bible. You have way too much at stake. And that's exactly why I am going to give you some instructions on how to use the Bible like a pro.

Where we're going next is the intersection where information collides with action in your life. As you wade into the Bible, I encourage you to start with the book of Proverbs in the Old Testament and Matthew in the New Testament. Here's why. Proverbs was written by Solomon, who, according to God's Word, is the wisest man to have ever lived. This book is all about wisdom. It's practical, it's relevant, and it's timeless. Proverbs has thirty-one chapters so it's easy to read a chapter a day that correlates with each day of the month. Think of it, you never need a bookmark, and you'll never loose your place as long as you know what day it is.

Matthew is the first of four eyewitness accounts of the life of Jesus Christ. There is no better way to begin moving closer to God than to read the accounts of the life of His one and only Son.

When you're getting started, don't underestimate the power in reading, contemplating, and praying about one chapter from Proverbs and one chapter from Matthew each day. This is a great way to start getting the Bible out of the driveway and onto the pavement.

So here's my disclaimer. If you'd rather start in other books of the Bible, that's your call as there is no right or wrong place to start reading it. The real issue is knowing what to do with what you read.

In the previous chapter I wrote that God guides and speaks to you about big decisions in your life as you read His Word. But how does that all work? Here are a few interesting things to consider.

As we read earlier, Psalm 119:105 says, "Your word is a lamp for my feet and a light on my path." God says that using the Bible is like using a lamp as you walk down a dark, unknown path. That's all well and good, but what's the key to this analogy? After all, God says the Bible is like a lamp, not like the sun or moonlight over our path. Why?

Think about it like this, if we're on that dark path and the light reflected off of the moon shone on our path exposing every danger or challenge, we wouldn't have to do anything to move forward. The light from the moon shines down regardless of whether we ever do anything, and our reliance on God and His plan for our lives would be void because we could see everything anyway.

Every lamp I've ever used had to be turned on first. I had to determine how to use it, or it wasn't going to light anything for me. In the same way a lamp has to be used properly in order to work, the Bible also has to be to used properly if we want light, or insight, from it. It has to be turned on, and nobody can do that for you except you. By grabbing that lamp and turning it on, you are putting some skin in the game.

So, how exactly can you use the Bible to let God speak and guide you today?

Have you ever used the pray-and-point technique? It's like buying lottery tickets to pay off your debts. A lot of people do it when they get in a jam or have a life question that needs to be answered. The scenario goes down like this: "God, I need to know if I should quit my job. You've got to tell me today. So I'm going to open the Bible, and the first thing I read is You telling me what to do." Then you close your eyes and start flipping wildly through the pages.

I picture that big wheel spinning on *The Price Is Right*, where the contestant yells, "Big money! Big money! Big money!" The pages of the Bible spin one way; we flip back the other way, one more spin forward, and a last huge flip backwards. At that point we close our eyes even tighter, reminding God one last time of this plan of ours. And then you slam your index finger down onto that "magical" verse and read it aloud: "He slaughtered the ox and the ram as the people's fellowship sacrifice" (Lev. 9:18).

"Oh, dear Lord! Is that for me, God? Because now I'm sort of scared."

Is that how it works? Flip through, point, and God speaks?

How Does God Speak through the Bible?

God will speak to us in obvious ways and in subtle ways, and it's our responsibility to listen for both. God's Word gives us clear instructions on many areas of life. It teaches us how to handle our money, relationships, priorities, forgiveness, and on and on. If we'll turn on the lamp (actually read the Bible), He'll guide us step-by-step.

You might ask, "Should I forgive that person even though she doesn't deserve it and has never even apologized?" The Bible says, "Be kind and compassionate to one another, forgiving one another, just as God also forgave you in Christ" (Eph. 4:32).

God's Word tells you what to do. He has made it obvious. You don't even have to ask Him. It's right there in black and white.

"Should I give back to God before or after I pay my personal bills?" "Honor the Lord with your possessions and with the first produce of your entire harvest" (Prov. 3:9–10). You don't need to pray about this question either.

"Should I break up with this person if they do not want to pursue God like I am?" "Do not be mismatched with unbelievers. For what partnership is there between righteousness and lawlessness? Or what fellowship does light have with darkness?" (2 Cor. 6:14).

Do you see the obvious ways God is already speaking to you through His Word?

"Should I put my spouse's dreams and desires above my own, or do what I want?" "Wives, be submissive to your husbands, as is fitting in the Lord" (Col. 3:18). "Husbands, love your wives, just as Christ loved the church and gave Himself for her" (Eph. 5:25).

Do you know how many divorces could be avoided if husbands and wives read just those two verses before making big decisions and actually did what they said to do?

"Should I lie in this situation? It's complicated; maybe I should." "A false witness will not go unpunished, and one who utters lies perishes" (Prov. 19:9).

"Cheat on my taxes?" "So it is a sin for the person who knows to do what is good and doesn't do it" (James 4:17).

The questions, and ultimately the answers, can go on and on.

We run to God and beg for answers about many issues. He's got to be looking down at us saying, "Are you serious? Stop asking Me these things. I've already told you; just turn on the lamp!"

The Bible allows God to speak to us about countless areas of our lives. The more time you spend in His Word, the more you will be aware of this, and the more often you'll experience God actually guiding and directing you through your life. This will impact your life and ultimately lead you to a stronger connection with Him.

But what about less obvious questions or decisions you need to make?

- Which job do I take?
- Should I go to school or go in another direction?
- Do I stay here or move?
- Is he the one?

When I was first told that God would guide me through big decisions, I remember thinking, *Really? I've never read the "quit your job at the bank, take the sales position, and move to Cleveland" verse!*

This is where communication with God gets fun! His Word is Him speaking, and spending time in it is us listening. Every time you open the Bible, you're opening up a conversation between you and God. You'll read a verse, and this little voice will go off inside of you saying, "That's for you today," or, "Pay attention to that." That still, small voice is God speaking to you. The more you have these conversations with God, the more familiar you become with His voice.

As you start reading a chapter of Matthew and a chapter of Proverbs each day, you'll come across certain parts, and you'll just know that it's for you. You'll know because that still voice of God is communicating directly to you through His living and active Word. The more you open yourself up for such experiences, the more it will happen. In fact, a good rule of thumb is to read the Bible each day until you get that small voice going off inside your head saying, "Yep, see that, that's for you today!" If you're two chapters into your daily Bible reading and haven't heard God's voice, then read on. It won't take long for you to get that sense of "this part is for me." And knowing you're going to read until you get a thought like that will help you stay focused while reading. Win-win.

The more you do this, the more accustomed you will become with hearing the voice of God as you read the Bible. Since your Bible reading will most likely be in a quiet place, you'll start getting used to hearing His voice in the quiet.

Here's the cool part about this. The more familiar you become with God's voice in privacy, the more you'll recognize it in chaos! And while hearing God's voice in our quiet bedroom is helpful, recognizing His voice in the middle of a fast-paced chaotic life is what we really need. So let me say again, the more familiar you become with God's voice in privacy, the more you'll recognize it in chaos.

Let me give you an example. I'm a huge sports fan, and one day my wife and I went to Wrigley Field in downtown Chicago for a Cubs game. Simply visiting Wrigley will bring a sports fan closer to God! The seventh-inning stretch rolled around (it's a time when the game stops and the entire crowd sings "Take Me Out to the Ball Game"). I'm in the hotdog line during the song, and the air is filled with thousands of fans screaming, "One, two, three strikes you're out at the old ball game." Within earshot I hear the soda vendor barking about his ice-cold drinks. Another man is yelling, "Popcorn, Beer here!" A mom is yelling for her kid, drunken guys are high-fiving one another, and people are carrying on. It's complete pandemonium. What I didn't know is that my wife had walked up behind me, and she's a gentle person with a soft voice, and she softly says, "Hey, honey." Immediately I spun around, knowing who it was and that she was talking to me.

How's that possible? In the middle of complete chaos, how could I hear her small, quiet voice? I mean, she didn't even say my name? I just knew it was her. See, I've heard her voice so many times in private, I recognize it in chaos!

That's how strong the connection should be between you and God. Many of us make big decisions on the fly in the midst of our chaotic lives. It's crucial that we hear His voice on the run, in the middle of chaos.

That's why we read the Bible! Every time we do so, we're learning the sound of the voice of God. We're becoming familiar with His leading during quiet times, so we'll recognize it in chaotic times. Before we know it, we're being guided on a daily basis by the Creator of the universe.

That's how we move closer to our dreams! That's how we move closer to our God! And that's what being in transit is all about! I told you this is where it gets good!

Each day, get into this God-ordained, spiritual vehicle, and do so with this phrase in mind: Read it. Write it. Do it!

Read It

Before you start your day, simply ask God to speak to you through His Word and then be confident, knowing He will! "'It is written: Man must not live on bread alone but on every word that comes from the mouth of God'" (Matt. 4:4).

Write It

Simplify and identify exactly what God is saying to you today. Get a notebook, a journal, use a Word document, whatever works for you; but don't stop reading until you can write down one thing God is saying to you through His Word. "The LORD answered me: Write down this vision; clearly inscribe it on tablets so one may easily read it" (Hab. 2:2).

Do It

Put God's instructions into action. Each day finish your reading time by asking God to help you do whatever He's asking you to do. This is where life-change happens! "In the same way faith, if it doesn't have works, is dead by itself" (James 2:17).

Operating this vehicle isn't nearly as difficult as it seems. Keep reading, or start reading a chapter of Matthew and a chapter of Proverbs, and allow God to speak to you. As you come across something that seems to apply to you, or you get that little voice in your head that says, "Pay attention to that," or, "That's for you," assume this is what God is saying to you today. Then write it down and ask God to help you live it out.

That's it: Read it. Write it. Do it! As any pilot will tell you, after you know what you're doing, all of those toggle switches and gauges aren't that difficult.

- You know what the Bible is.
- You know what it can do for you.
- You know how to start operating it.

Get excited! Know that your communication with God is about to go to new heights. This vehicle will take you closer to God than you've ever been before. The only thing left to do now is do it. It's time for you to "take off." Enjoy the flight!

Vehicle 3

Relationships

Chapter 10

Go Live with Your Mom

Believe it or not, your relationship with God is not just about you and God. I grew up hearing people say things like, "It's nobody else's business, it's just between me and God." Then turn around and use that line of thinking as an excuse on why they didn't go to church or spend time with Christ followers. They felt it had nothing to do with anything, or anyone, else. I heard that more times than I can remember, and it actually doesn't sound all that bad unless you actually read what God has to say about it. God makes clear that getting closer to Him will require you to use the relationship vehicle He's given to us. And I will admit I learned the hard way that my relationship with God is not just about the two of us.

In the weeks after I planned my suicide, a lot happened. I had gone from the depths of despair thinking about killing myself to a church in Rockford asking God to take over my life. Throw in my baptism and three weeks of abstaining from everything sinful in my life, and presto, I was a new man.

But now I had come full circle and was back in Hollywood as a full-fledged, card-carrying Christian. Is that what I was? I didn't even know what to call myself at the time. But what I did know was that I had given up all the fun I used to have (girls, drugs, and booze), and abstaining from them was killing me. They made me feel good, yet really bad at the same time.

I felt good knowing my life had changed. I was going to heaven, and I was a better version of me than I used to be. But I felt bad because I wanted to be instantly closer to God; yet I still couldn't figure out how exactly to make that happen. I'd pray often, but my prayers were short and mostly just me complaining to Him. I had tried to read the Bible regularly, but the confusion I encountered put an end to that. The last straw being my time in the café on Melrose Avenue.

So there I was, three weeks into my new life and not a clue what to do next. I wanted to be closer to God but had no idea how to make that happen.

One Friday night, when the biggest agenda item for the evening was deciding which frozen dinner I'd eat, I sat at home and watched TV by myself . . . again! Greg, my closest friend and roommate, had enough of my social decline. He was genuinely worried about me. After all, living in Hollywood was my idea. I was the one who wanted to go out every night. I was the one who got us in trouble most of the time. I was the one who needed someone to slow me down. And now I had relegated myself to the couch while Greg was left to navigate the Hollywood nightlife without a wingman.

"Come on Johnson, let's go out," he said. "You don't even have to drink since apparently you don't do that anymore."

"Nah, I'm staying here."

"It'll do you good to get off that couch," he countered. "Come on, we'll just go shoot some pool, nothing else."

I considered his words. This conversation had become routine, and I was quickly running out of excuses.

"Nothing but pool, right?"

"Yeah, you nun! Let's go!"

Convincing myself a little game of pool wasn't going to keep me out of heaven, I jumped into the shower, got dressed, and made my way with Greg to our favorite pool hall in Hollywood.

As soon as we arrived, Greg ordered a beer, and I opted for a glass of water, determined not to slide back into my old ways. We commenced in our normal routine of playing pool at an average level and talking trash at a near professional level.

After a few games Greg said, "Let me buy you just one beer, man."

"Nah, I don't really want one," I said, lying through my teeth. I was dying for a beer, and watching him drink was torture.

"Come on, just one. What will it hurt?"

"Oh sure, just one," I said, giving in way too easily. "One beer isn't going to hurt anyone. Sure, why not?"

One won't hurt. If you've ever dealt with a substance abuse problem, you already know where this is headed. *Two's no big deal, and heck, what's the difference between two and three beers?*

After the fourth beer I realized I was at the point of no return so I ordered another one . . . and another one, and before I knew it, Greg left but was replaced by some of my more serious party friends. Greg never joined me on the path of hardcore drugs and knew little about my addictions. Isn't it crazy how much we can hide from the people we love the most?

Apparently word had spread with my other group of friends that I had come back to life and was ready to get back in the game of partying. Before I knew it, I was standing in a bathroom stall staring at a bag of cocaine. I remember thinking, *I'm a changed man, and I don't do this stuff anymore.* But I'd already drunk way past excess, so cocaine didn't seem like that big a deal either, and besides God was all about forgiveness, right? I convinced myself that He'd understand. But just to be safe, I decided not to do an entire line of coke—that's what godless people do. I'd just do a key bump, the amount of cocaine I could scoop out of the bag with my car key.

My memories of the night's events get fuzzy at this point. I do remember going to a club where I met a girl. We did drugs in the parking lot, in the bathroom, and then sitting in a booth just off the dance floor. I did whatever drugs were available and as much as I could get my hands on. I impressed myself with how many drugs I consumed. At some point later that girl and I went back to my place. About an hour after that, I was standing in front of the mirror in my bathroom, crying, trying to keep my balance, and hating everything about myself.

As I told you earlier, I just kept asking myself, "This is what a Christian looks like, huh?"

After puking into the toilet several times, I made my way back to my room and went to sleep. I woke up the next morning, my guest had already left, and the phone was ringing. I don't know why I even answered it, but with a groggy, raspy telltale voice, I did. "Hello."

"Shawn?" asked the woman on the other end of the phone. "It's Jeanne, from Rockford."

Jeanne was Eric's boss at the church in Rockford. She was the pastor's wife and director of all the young adult ministries at the church. She was also the last person I wanted to talk to in my hungover state.

"I was just calling to see how you're doing," she said.

A few hours removed from the hardest night of partying I'd ever experienced, and I had the pastor's wife calling me to ask how my Christianity is holding up!

God does have a sense of humor, I thought, *or He's just mad at me.*

Sensing I was cornered, I decided to come clean. Honestly, I was too tired and too sick to lie about my current state so I just told her everything that happened the night before. As I recounted the events, I became convinced I was going straight to hell for telling a pastor's wife these sorts of things.

"Look Jeanne, I tried my hardest to give this Christian thing a shot, but I just don't have what it takes," I said. "I'm sorry!"

I remember tearing up as I said, "I just can't do it."

Have you ever felt that way? No matter how hard you try, you just can't seem to measure up as a follower of Christ. You go to church, and look around the room, and think, *I could never be like these people; they're good, and I'm not.*

No matter how long you've been trying to follow God, a little voice in the back of your mind is saying, "You're not good enough." You've got to know right now you are not alone. At different times for different reasons, we all struggle with thoughts like this about following God. It's normal; we're imperfect people trying to get close to a perfect God. It's bound to happen from time to time.

But here's the good news, you're not supposed to look like the people sitting around you in church! You didn't earn a relationship with God, and neither did any of the people you're comparing yourself to. Here's a fact you need to remember whenever you don't feel good enough: None of us are! None of us, no matter how many good things we do and say will ever be deserving of the forgiveness and grace and love Christ freely extends to us.

But here's a bit of good news, all of us can use the spiritual vehicles outlined in this book to move closer to God! We get to use these vehicles, and we get to experience a real relationship with God, and none of it is merit based. We don't have to earn anything, but we will have to decide if we're willing to use the means of transportation God has provided for us.

As Jeanne and I talked that day, she said something I'll never forget: "Shawn, you can do this, but the Bible says you have to flee from evil." She was referring to: "Flee from youthful passions, and pursue righteousness" (2 Tim. 2:22).

I'd never read that verse, but I knew what she meant. She went on to tell me that if I really wanted to get serious about pursuing God, I was going to have to make some relational changes in my life.

"Show me your friends, and I'll show you your future," she said. "Your close friends will either bring you closer to God or push you from Him. At the end of the day, you need to decide what you really want from this life."

"Well, what am I supposed to do?" I asked. "This is where I live, who I work with and do life with. What am I supposed to do?"

"Go live with your mom!" she said matter-of-factly.

I couldn't help but laugh. "She lives in Kansas!" I blurted. "Kansas is like Alcatraz; once you escape, you don't go back on purpose!" I don't think so!

"Then move to Rockford and live with Eric," she said without missing a beat. "You have to do something, Shawn. You've got to get around people who are heading in the same direction as you. You've got to get around other followers of Christ. Doing so will change everything for you because you can't do this on your own."

I was so hungover that arguing wasn't a possibility, so I thanked her for the call and hung up as quickly as I could.

Go live with your mom. Seriously? What's wrong with this lady? I thought.

I stumbled back to my bedroom and crawled back into bed. I wrapped myself into a cocoon of blankets and wished I could will my hangover away. A few hours later I woke up thinking about what Jeanne had said. To be honest, her words had been offensive to me. I loved my friends, and they loved me. It certainly wasn't their fault I lost control and did all the stupid things I had done. The fault was all mine.

As the day wore on, I couldn't help but wonder if it was possible that relationships in my life, although made up of some great people, were hindering me from getting closer to God. Not because I was in any way better than my friends but simply because I wanted to focus on being closer to God and they just didn't.

Is it possible you could be in the same situation today? Your friends might not be into alcohol or drugs, but is it possible that the voice they have in your life today is slowly dragging you farther and farther from the relationship with God you so badly desire?

This was definitely something I needed to get figured out for myself, and you will too.

Chapter 11

Why Does This Really Matter?

This relationship thing Jeanne was talking to me about was huge! And if I was going to act on what she was saying, it was going to flip my life upside down! To change the relationships in my life meant I had to change just about everything about me. So I had to ask myself the same hard question you might be asking right now, "Why does this really matter?"

The people closest to us in our lives are close to us because we like them! We trust them, we love them, and we've been through a lot with them. For some of us, our friends are closer to us than many family members. So even thinking that one or all of your friends might be holding you back from getting closer to God is in itself akin to an act of betrayal most of us can't imagine even considering.

But what do you do if your friends are keeping you from God?

First, don't freak out. Realize that if your friends are toxic to your relationship with God, you need to create some distance between you and them. This doesn't mean you should voice any judgment of your friends' character or integrity. You've just come to a crossroad in your life where you're headed in one direction that your friends aren't interested in going.

Here's some tough love you'll need to keep in mind as you go through this relational gauntlet: just because you decided to follow Christ as your Savior, doesn't mean God loves you more than He loves your friends. But you might need to separate for a little while so that your relationship with God can get stronger.

Think of it like this: if you're going to dinner and you want Mexican and your best friend is dead set on pizza, a decision has to be made. Do you want to hang out with your friend, or do you really want to go get Mexican? You can't do both. If your heart's desire is to eat Mexican and you believe it's going to be the best thing for you, it's time to order some tacos and hand-rolled burritos.

I had to decide: Do I want to hang out with my friends, or do I want to move closer to God because I can't do both at the same time? You won't be able to either, sorry.

About now is when you'll start trying to convince yourself that your situation is different. Those close to you are different because they're so nice and caring and loving, and although not followers of Christ, they would never purposely try to keep you from your pursuit of God. Besides that, you're strong enough to make sure that never happens. Before you know it, in your mind you will become a world-class defense attorney, and you'll do about anything to justify your toxic relationships. But listen—right now, you are at a paramount crossroads in your life, and the next few decisions you make will determine your future.

You must remind yourself: you are not above the law. God will not be mocked with our futile explanations of why our situation is so "different," and this just doesn't fall under His guidelines. He has made abundantly clear that our relationships will determine our proximity to Him and the plans He has for us.

> Do not be yoked together with unbelievers. For what do righteousness and wickedness have in common? Or what fellowship can light have with darkness? (2 Cor. 6:14 NIV)

Understanding this visual analogy will help bring some clarity to this entire line of thinking. Backtrack with me for a second. When the apostle Paul wrote 2 Corinthians, the people who heard his words knew exactly what he meant when he said, "Do not be yoked together with unbelievers." Yokes and oxen back then were like Toyotas or Fords today. Many people worked in or lived on what we would call the agriculture industry. Simply put, almost everyone was a farmer or knew someone that was.

A yoke is a wooden device that couples two oxen that are attached to a plow. Both of the oxen would put their heads through the yoke, be strapped in, and be ready to hit the road. The oxen can be controlled easier this way, allowing the farmer to plow straight ahead down each row of a field. As every good farmer or kid from Kansas knows, the oxen need to be equal in strength for the plow to go straight. If one ox is strong and the other is weak, the stronger ox will pull his side of the yoke faster, forcing the plow off its path.

Think of it like this: it doesn't matter where the farmer wants to end up; if one of the oxen is weaker than the other, the farmer, plow, and oxen will not reach their intended destination. Although they all may want to go straight, their direction will suffer because of the differences in strength between the two animals.

Our lives work the same way. God has a specific path He has tailor-made for you. He doesn't want you to miss the mark because something or someone gently pulls you away. "Carefully consider the path for your feet, and all your ways will be established. Don't turn to the right or to the left; keep your feet away from evil" (Prov. 4:26–27).

This verse says something you need to notice. It's your choice whether you stay on the right path, and that has everything to do with the decisions you make here and now.

Through the analogy of the ox and the yoke, I believe God is telling us that if we decide to connect ourselves to a nonbeliever, regardless of how much you love that person and regardless of how badly you want to go down a straight path, the person you love will pull you off course. If that happens, it can cost you your God-given future. That's heavy stuff. Regardless of who the person is and how far you go back with him or her, no relationship is worth missing out on the plans God has for you!

Relationships, when used properly, will each day move you closer to God. The people whom you spend time with, or don't spend time with, are crucial because your God-given future is on the line. Your relationships will dictate way more than just what you do next weekend.

It would do us all a lot of good to filter each of our relationships through this statement: "The one who walks with the wise will become wise, but a companion of fools will suffer harm" (Prov. 13:20).

God says *wise* counsel in this life will point you in the right direction, but getting *foolish* counsel will not only point you in the wrong direction, but you will suffer harm because of it. Godly friends help us get closer to God.

Ungodly friends take us farther from God and, as a result, cause us to "suffer harm."

One night I was having dinner with my wife, Jill, and our three young sons: Ethan, Austin, and Ashton. Austin says, "Hey Mom, if I eat my green beans first, how will I have room for dessert?" Before Jill could answer, our youngest, who reminds me of a miniature drunk at times, repeats his older brother at the top of his lungs. "Yeah Mom, if I eat my gween beans fist, I won't have womb for desset!"

If the only counsel Austin ever got came from his little brother, he'll be eating cheesecake before vegetables for the rest of his life! Counsel only helps when it's *wise* counsel. The problem for most of us is that we'd rather ask our friends (whether they are wise or not) for input into our lives. And why would we do that? For the same reasons we don't think they'd ever drag us away from a relationship with God. Because they are our friends! We love them, they love us; we trust them and they trust us. But a good friend does not always equal wise counsel!

"The one who walks with the wise will become wise, but a companion of fools will suffer harm" (Prov. 13:20). You know what that verse says, "Stop asking your stupid friends for advice!"

I know that sounds harsh, but its true. A good friend does not always make for "wise counsel."

And what I'm about to say, I wish someone had said to me a long time ago! Stop asking your maxed-out credit card, broke friends for financial advice. Stop asking your video-game playing, unemployed friends for career advice. Stop asking your unhappily married friends for marriage advice. Stop asking your atheist friends for religious advice. Stop asking your heartbroken friends for dating advice. I could go on here, but you get the point.

One of the worst ones I've seen recently was a great couple who were contemplating divorce. The husband decided to reach out to a recently divorced friend of his. He asked his newly divorced friend if he should fight for the marriage or throw in the towel. I'm sure his buddy was the nicest, most sincere best friend a guy could ever want, but at that moment in time, he was not in a position to give wise counsel. The outcome was heart breaking.

Even though we all know our best friends do not always give wise counsel, we keep going to them for help on the biggest decisions of our lives. You do it and I do it because we love them, and if we were completely honest, because we know they'll probably tell us what we want to hear, not what we need to hear.

If you get bad advice and it takes you down a path you never really wanted to go down, no one suffers but you! So, while you are trying to move closer to God, cut your losses and build some separation between you and your old friends who don't know God. It will be painful, but it will also improve your odds of making the right decisions early in your faith.

God says He'll speak to you about big decisions in life through wise counsel so it's crucial you get this right. The question is: What does wise counsel look like? And God says, "I thought you'd never ask." Here's a start: "The fear of the LORD is the beginning of wisdom, and the knowledge of the Holy One is understanding" (Prov. 9:10).

God tells us that wise counsel starts with the fear of God. Not with high IQ points. Not with money. Not with one's social status. Not with success in a particular field. All those things have currency in our culture, but unfortunately they do not determine wise counsel. Wise counsel comes from wisdom, which starts with the fear of God! It's that simple.

I have nonbelieving friends with incredibly high IQs as well as believing friends with incredibly high IQs. If my future is on the line, if it's going to affect my family, I'm hitting up my friends who know Christ for wise counsel. The reason I don't defer to my nonbelieving friends is because they don't make decisions with God in mind, and that's not the direction I want to go. Because they don't live their lives with God in mind, I don't want their advice on the things that *really* matter!

Here's how you can spot a wise, godly counselor:

- Their pursuit of God is evident, even to the point where you might think, *I wish my pursuit after God looked like theirs.*
- They're sold-out followers of Jesus Christ. They're not perfect, but they're doing their best to serve and honor God.
- They're unbiased when it comes to you and your decision.
- They're comfortable enough with you to be brutally honest.
- They could care less about impressing you.
- They have your best interests in mind.
- They have nothing to lose or gain by the outcome of your decision.

If your friends have the aforementioned attributes, you'll regularly see the benefits of the collision of understanding and wisdom coming from their words, actions, and lives. These are the kind of people you want to surround you when you need godly advice.

Relationships matter because they affect your destination in life and in eternity. They will influence you, taking you closer to God. "And let us be concerned about one another in order to promote love and good works" (Heb. 10:24).

Throughout the Bible, God is referred to as Love. In Hebrews, we are implored to spur one another toward Love [God]. Go IRS on your relationships and ask yourself if they are all spurring and pushing you toward God. Do a relational audit. If there are relationships that might separate you from God, then separate yourself from them.

"Iron sharpens iron, and one man sharpens another" (Prov. 27:17). Our God-honoring relationships will include people who make us wiser and push us toward Him. James, the half brother of Jesus, said this about our relationships: "Therefore, confess your sins to one another and pray for one another, so that you may be healed" (James 5:16).

James is describing what godly relationships look like. Ask yourself a few questions: "Am I comfortable with those closest to me to confess sins and weaknesses? Would my friends then pray with me about life's biggest challenges? Do my friends encourage me to grow closer to God?"

If the answer is no to any of these questions, you have some soul searching to do. Those closest to you should do all those things and more for you.

Remember your situation is not different and there are no neutral relationships. Every relationship you currently have is taking you somewhere, and it's either toward God or away from Him.

Chapter 12

What Should I Do Now?

Once we understand the importance of relationships, we'll want to get everything out of them we can. We'll want our relationships to propel us toward an authentic connection with God and even with other followers of Christ. So, what now? We have the friends we have. We work where we work. We're close to the people we're close to. So, what do we do now?

Depending on where you land with all of this, you may have to make some tough decisions. I did. One of the toughest questions I had to ask myself was, "Do I want to hang out with this person, or do I want a life-altering relationship with Creator God?" For me the decision was difficult but obvious. I wanted to be closer to God so I had to create separation with some of my friends so spiritually I didn't die. That's what is at stake here. So with love, honesty, transparency, and sincerity, I made some relational adjustments.

You'll have to do the same if you want to be closer to God than you are today. Simply put, you need to get out of the wrong relationships and get into the right ones: Simple . . . yes. Easy . . . no.

It won't be easy, but here are some action steps to help you along this difficult part of the journey.

Action Step 1: Get Out of the Wrong Relationships

You might already be thinking what I am proposing here is crazy. I don't blame you. And no, I am not asking you to sever all communication and ties to the people you love. I am asking you to put some distance between you and your old friends who don't believe like you do. Let me put this in context. Earlier I mentioned my buddy and roommate, Greg. He was and is one of the best people I've ever met. But when I committed my life to Christ, he just wasn't interested in doing the same thing at that time, so my relationship with him had to change. I had to create some separation to keep moving toward God. But know this, years later Greg was the best man in my wedding, and I'll always cherish our friendship.

We should be friends with nonbelievers. We should be reaching out to and extending love to nonbelievers, but the relationships with those people must look and operate differently from ones we have with followers of Christ. But what if you're married to a nonbeliever? For the sake of brevity, just know that God will give you the strength to honor your spouse and continue to work on his or her heart as you continue to show your spouse love and support. That said, a nonbeliever (who is not your spouse) should never influence any of your major life decisions.

The best example of towing the line between friends who are believers and those who are not is Jesus. He lived in a community with believers, then visited nonbelievers with the purpose of ministering to them, and then He would go back to "doing life" with believers. Here are a couple things Jesus did that you should emulate:

- His best friends were believers.
- His soul mates were believers.
- He "did life" with believers.
- He spent time with lost people for a strategic amount of time with a strategic purpose.

Let me break this down for you. We should do life with other Christ followers and visit the world with purpose. The problem for many of us today, especially when we start following Christ, is that we do the opposite of what Jesus did. We do life with the world and visit Christ followers once a week with purpose. Does this profile seem familiar to you:

- Our best friends are nonbelievers.
- We date nonbelievers.
- We confide in and ask for advice from nonbelievers.
- We visit Christ followers on Sunday for church.

If the above resembles your situation today, you have to make a change if you ever want your relationships to help you move into a life-changing relationship with God.

We should do life with other Christ followers and visit the world with purpose. Good intentions are not enough. We have to be proactive. We have to take action. You can do this—you can operate this spiritual vehicle, and here's how:

- Make a tough phone call.
- Break up.
- Move out.
- Change jobs.
- Stay home on the weekends.
- Go live with your mother if necessary!

It's tough to do the above, but when you do, you'll find out who your real friends are. Real friends truly care about you and will understand your need to move closer to God. They will understand that you need to head in a different direction.

Some of my party friends were never to be heard from again the moment I told them I was seriously going to pursue God. I understood why—our relationship was a lot of

TRANSIT

smoke and mirrors filled with common interests and nice-
ties. In other words, the friendship was a mile wide but an
inch deep. That wasn't so with Greg. Although he didn't
tag along at the time, Greg understood and supported my
decision to pursue Jesus. He didn't really get what I was trying to do, but he didn't write me off because of it. Making
relational adjustments will help you weed through your
relationships, and you'll quickly see those who really care
about you because they will rise to the top. Regardless of
anyone else's reaction, keep in mind that this journey is all
about you moving closer to God.

Now for some easy stuff. You absolutely need to get
involved in a local church.

If you want to build relationships with the right people,
you've got to start putting yourself in the right places. Going
to the bar and hoping to make some good Christian friends
probably isn't the fastest route to the relationships you seek.
Going to a local church is not a suggestion; it's a must-do
agenda item for your life.

Once you get through the doors of your local, Bible-
believing church, you need to get into a small group. Many
churches have groups that focus on areas of interest such as
sports, parenting, motorcycles, cooking, and Bible study. It's
one of the best ways to make new friends and guarantees
you'll see people you know on Sunday mornings.

Then you need to find every opportunity to be around the people in that church. One of the best ways to do that is to volunteer. Every church in America needs people who will greet people at the door, usher, work in the children's area, or even do janitorial work.

To give this vehicle the rocket fuel it needs to scream down the road of life, you can't be a nonparticipant; you have to get on the road and make some moves to make some new friends.

Just so you know, I do not consider myself someone who has arrived spiritually. Life is full of twists and turns, and I have not always negotiated each hairpin perfectly. In fact, as I look back at my life, I think I've done more things wrong than I've ever done right. Truth is, I was nothing more than a messed-up kid wanting the same things in life you want. I wanted to be loved, I wanted to feel wanted, I wanted to live with a purpose; and one day I blinked and realized that a relationship with God was the ticket to such a life.

The morning Jeanne, the pastor's wife from Rockford, called me, I knew I had to make some tough decisions that would either make or break me. I was desperate for a change in life, and I decided that morning that I wanted to be closer to God more than I wanted to spend time partying. So I called my producer and said I was quitting, again. Then I told my best friend and roommate, Greg, I was moving to Rockford. I had come to a point of my life where

I didn't care what my friends thought of me. I was going to get closer to God if it killed me.

Almost immediately I packed three cardboard boxes full of clothes, hopped on a plane to Illinois, and moved into Parks's tiny, two-bedroom apartment. Well, actually I moved into their enclosed porch that didn't have heat or air-conditioning. For any Chris Farley fans, an enclosed porch was one small step up from a van down by the river! I had no more pride, no more money, no real plans other than getting closer to Jesus and other Christ followers.

Of course I was scared, humbled, nervous, and completely confused, but for some reason I knew I was on the right path. I had a surreal confidence that I was finally running all out toward God and that from now on He'd be in charge of my life.

And He was!

I met my wife in a small group at the church. (I told you, you've got to get in one of these!) From that small group I also learned leadership skills and discovered that I wanted to spend my life helping others move closer to God. In short order I became an intern at the church and eventually a pastor. Talk about confusing. My old friends still can't believe it!

Fast-forward to today. I'm still married to Jill, we have three sons, and I'm pastoring a great church where I get to see thousands of people experience the life-changing power of God every week. My life isn't perfect by any means, but it's a dream come true for me. I love my family, and they love me in return. I live with real purpose and passion for life, which I never had before. I spend so much time thanking God these days for the miraculous life-change He's allowed me to experience and that I am still experiencing today.

Here is something crazy to consider. If I hadn't bailed on L.A., my acting career, and all the "friends" I partied with, I would have missed out on all God has provided. That's scary to consider. If I hadn't moved away from what was comfortable, I would have never met Jill. I wouldn't have had my three boys. I would not be a pastor. And I wouldn't live where I now live and get to do all I love to do. One decision to honor God with my relationships changed my entire future.

I didn't walk away from my old friends and a way of living because I was smarter than everyone else. But today I am so thankful for so many things, the biggest being that I decided to create some space between myself and my old friends so that I could move closer to Jesus. Doing so has changed everything about my life!

The same can happen for you today! You just have to be willing to make a tough decision and act on it. If you do, you'll never regret it!

Vehicle 4

Serving

Chapter 13

A Proud Funeral

y life-changing journey began on the balcony of my Hollywood apartment. As I questioned my life, what it stood for, and why it did or didn't matter to anyone else, the answers started to scare me.

It scared me because I realized I had no purpose in life, and I remember thinking, *Even though I have lots of friends, most of them wouldn't be that upset if I died tomorrow.* They'd be sad for a few hours but probably would then go party just like every other night. Nobody would really miss me if I were gone because my life was really only about me.

Mother Teresa once said, "One of the greatest diseases is to be nobody to anybody." Back then that summed up my entire life. I was definitely nobody to anybody, and that fact hurt in ways I never thought possible until I was standing on the balcony surveying my life.

Let me ask you a tough question: Have you ever wondered if your life really matters to anyone else? And by anyone else I mean people outside your family who aren't forced to give you the benefit of the doubt. On the balcony that day, I couldn't help but think: *Does my life matter?*

Today I know the answer. Back then I didn't, and maybe right now you don't. God has a lot to say to you about your life today: "For we are His creation, created in Christ Jesus for good works, which God prepared ahead of time so that we should walk in them" (Eph. 2:10).

I'll translate that for you into my words: God created you with a very specific purpose in mind. He has a plan for your life. That plan will afford you opportunities to honor God, serve others, and experience purpose on a level you never had before. That's exactly why I want to introduce you to the vehicle of serving. It changes everything.

Before I committed my life to Christ, I couldn't have been expected to have a desire to serve other people. Like many people who don't know Jesus, my life revolved around me and only me. I spent all my time and effort trying to get girls, money, and status. I was trying to feel successful and happy. Yet all those things proved to be fleeting because no matter how much I attained, I never felt really fulfilled, and I kept returning to this thought: *Is this all there is to life?*

As strange as this may sound, that question got me thinking about my funeral. For the life of me, I couldn't help but wonder who would come and what they would say. I imagined my immediate family sitting in a neat row, waiting for a turn to speak about me. Would my loved ones and friends tell funny stories, relive fond memories, and confess how much they'd miss me? I wasn't sure. That put a twinge of fear in me, but then I shifted into an all-out panic mode when I considered what would happen if someone opened the funeral mic up to the public at large. I imagined one of my children saying, "Now if anyone would like to talk about what my dad meant to you, step up to the mic and do so now."

Would anyone come running to the mic because I had positively changed their life to the point that they just had to share it?

Would there be any stories of me sacrificing for them and how it meant the world to them?

Could someone drum up a story of a time when I was generous beyond belief?

Would there be any record of times when I served other people?

The answer to all those questions was simple—no.

If I had died that day on the balcony, I would not have had what I would call a "proud funeral." I just simply had not put in enough time, effort, or resources into serving other people.

Today as a pastor (I still cringe a little when I say that) going to funerals is a part of my job. Out of all the funerals I've been to over the years, I've never seen anyone run to the mic to celebrate all the money the dead person made. Nobody gets choked up talking about how their life was changed because the deceased had an amazing house or a beautiful car collection. I've never heard, "She changed my life because she worked so many hours and spent so much time investing in her career." It just never happens. After officiating many funerals, I've come to the conclusion that there are funerals and then there are proud funerals.

The standard funeral is not filled with lots of stories about the great things the deceased did. Tears are usually in short supply, and time passes so slowly because everyone is scrambling to find something of note to say.

At a proud funeral the stories, shared memories, and recounting of generosity, humbleness, and kindness fill what feels like the precious few hours dedicated to the mourning of such a great person.

"My life was changed because he sacrificed for me by . . ."

"I'll never forget her because she would always help people who couldn't help themselves by . . ."

"He changed my life because he went out of his way to show me love when he . . ."

When someone dies, status and stuff become meaningless. The only thing that matters is how the deceased served others. At the core of who we are, we want to make a difference in other people's lives, and we want to be remembered as doing such. We want to be remembered for the *stories* of life-change that happened because of what we did.

Jesus knows exactly how we feel and exactly what we crave. In Mark 9, Jesus' best friends, the disciples, are having a heated discussion about this very topic. They ask who will be closest to Jesus and who would be remembered as being great. Jesus knows what they're talking about. He knows what they desire, so He huddles with them for a group discussion.

> And he sat down and called the twelve. And he said to them, "If anyone would be first, he must be last of all and servant of all." (Mark 9:35 ESV)

Imagine Jesus at the center of this huddle. All the guys are looking intently at Him, hoping He will single one of them out as the greatest. But it doesn't go like that. "Look guys," He says, if He spoke like me, "I know what you want, but you're going about it all wrong. You're seeking status and stuff, and you should be looking for serving opportunities to create stories. If you want to be truly great, you have to start serving others."

"And whoever would be first among you must be slave of all. For even the Son of Man came not to be served but to serve, and to give his life as a ransom for many." (Mark 10:44–45 ESV)

"Look at it from where I'm at," Jesus continues. "I'm not telling you to do something I'm not doing Myself. I came to this world to serve. In fact, I'll be giving My life in order to serve you. If you want to be great, if you want the best possible life, if you want a life that matters, well, you've got to start serving other people."

I truly believe that if Jesus were huddling with us right now, He would tell us the same thing because serving others brings us purpose, it makes us truly great, and it changes our lives and the lives of the people we serve. Even more important, it takes us closer to God.

We were created to serve others through good works.

Just after moving to Rockford, Parks told me I had to get into a small group. At first I balked at the idea. First, I didn't have the church-issue khakis everyone seemed to have. Second, I wasn't sure if I was going to fit in; and third, I had no idea what activities would comprise a small-group meeting. To my surprise, all of my fears were unfounded. No one in the small group cared that I wasn't wearing khakis. Everyone was pretty cool, and I learned quickly that followers of Christ know how to have a good time even without drugs and booze. At the time I was way too cool to admit how much I enjoyed my small group.

During that first small-group meeting we looked at a verse that spoke of being a servant: "The greatest among you will be your servant" (Matt. 23:11).

This verse instantly made sense to me. In an instant it brought clarity and condemnation for all the years I'd spent thinking only of me. The Hollywood life encouraged self-centeredness and the notion that the more people who served you, the more important you were. Being great was measured by how many people asked, "How high?" the second you said, "Jump!"

I worked with movie stars who arrived on set in a three-limousine cavalcade. People opened doors for them, catered to their every need, did their hair and makeup for them, set up their trailer for them, got them every brand of water they demanded and as many green M&Ms as they could eat. For a time in my life, I wanted to be the movie star everyone wished they could do things for. I had bought hook, line, and sinker into the idea that the greater I was, the more I should be served.

In a matter of weeks, I moved from Hollywood to the middle of the country and found myself sitting in a small group discussing a verse that crushed everything I'd lived for and everything I'd dreamed of. Let's face it, at one time or another, we've all wanted the movie-star treatment. Isn't it true, we've all dreamed of being the professional athlete, the star of the show, or the CEO? Haven't we all imagined how nice it would be to have people serving our every whim? But this passage of Scripture messes all of that up.

Jesus is right and the world is wrong. The proudest funerals are the ones where people can't stop talking about how you served them. The greatest among us really are the servants in this world.

Jesus was teaching His best friends then and us today. Greatness is defined by actions, not status and stuff. I'll never forget the first time I saw this lived out.

Several years ago a friend named Jared called early in the morning and asked if I'd meet him and his wife, Jalah, because Jalah's mother had passed away the night before. I was new to the whole pastor thing and scared to death. As I drove to her house, I wondered: *What do I do? What do I say? Do I pray with them?*

Upon arrival at their home, I realized my main job was just to be there. We talked, hugged, cried, and eventually even prayed. At one point, as I was talking to some of the family members in the kitchen, my attention was seized by the sheer number of photographs on the refrigerator. There were so many I wondered if a fridge was really even under all of them.

"Who are all these people?" I asked incredulously, expecting to hear about kids, grandkids, nephews, and nieces.

"Just people Theresa has helped through the years," said one of Jalah's relatives.

"Huh? You mean like family members she helped?"

"Some of them are family," said the relative as she joined me in gazing in awe at the multitude of people represented in the photos. "But most of them are just people around town or around the neighborhood that she's helped. That's just who Theresa was. She was always helping people."

Theresa's fridge was a monument to the power of serving others. Picture after picture, person after person, young, old, related, not related. I was completely moved by this sight. As I drove home, I couldn't help but think about that refrigerator and all the pictures of random people Theresa had served.

Later that week I was amazed when I saw the enormous crowd of people at her funeral. Like most of the other guests, I cried the entire time. Story after story of how Theresa did this or that to help others filled the church and our hearts. Theresa's life was one that was lived out of the spotlight and with little regard for the world's priorities. But what an impact it made on those she served.

As we said good-bye to Theresa, I remember thinking, *I hope my children are this proud of me someday.* The funny thing is, not once did anyone talk about how much money was in Theresa's savings account or the square footage of her house or how nice her car was. All that mattered was that she loved her neighbors by serving them. I can only hope my life is worthy enough to have a funeral like Theresa Spiller someday because it was a proud funeral.

Chapter 14

Greatness Can Be Bought

F or me it was on a balcony. Maybe for you it was while reading the last chapter. But at some point every one of us will come face-to-face with the reality of what our life is currently about, where it is taking us, and how we'll be remembered because of it. We're not the first people to think about this stuff. People have been thinking about this and asking about this for thousands of years.

One day Jesus said: "Love the Lord your God with all your heart, with all your soul, and with all your mind. This is the greatest and most important command. The second is like this: Love your neighbor as yourself" (Matt. 22:37–39).

A couple thousand years ago the aforementioned statement was discussed by some people who wanted the same things we want out of life. They wanted to be close to God, and they wanted to live a life that really mattered, so someone asked Jesus, "Who is my neighbor?" (Luke 10:29).

The guy asking the question was basically saying he wanted to live a Theresa Spiller-type life, but how? And who exactly is that neighbor you speak of, Jesus?

In response to this Jesus tells His followers a story about a man traveling from Jerusalem to Jericho. On the way some robbers attacked the man and beat him half to death. The thieves take everything he has, including his clothes, and leave him to die on the side of the road. When a priest and a Levite walk by this bloodied body, having everything they needed to help this man, they pass by without helping. Yet, when a Samaritan passes by and sees that the man is in need, he responds in kindness. He bandages the man's wounds, takes him to town, gets him a place to stay, and pays all the bills. Jesus says, "If you want to be my disciple, if you want to live a life of purpose, if you want to be close to God the Father, then, 'go and do the same'" (Luke 10:37).

The Samaritan saw a need and acted in love. The lesson you need to walk away with is that if you see someone in need, help them! It's called serving, and it's one of the greatest vehicles you'll ever operate. "Let us not love with words or speech but with actions and in truth" (1 John 3:18 niv).

Loving God's way isn't lip service; it's real service! But be warned, it's easy to talk yourself out of serving others.

We Talk Ourselves Out of Serving Others

Maybe the priest and the Levite are guilty of nothing more than talking themselves out of a good opportunity to serve someone who is desperately in need. It's just a theory, but these fellas handled temple worship so in a way, serving others is in their career DNA. So, why would they pass by someone who obviously needed help?

Perhaps they thought the man was dead. If so, they would have been exercising wisdom by not getting involved because, as leaders who handled temple worship, they were not allowed to touch dead people or even get near unclean people. If they did, they'd have to go through public cleansing rituals before they could go back to work inside the temple.

I bet they wanted to help; they were good, God-fearing people. But I also bet they talked themselves out of doing so.

Maybe he's dead. I can't touch a dead man.

Maybe's he's unclean. I can't associate with certain kinds of people.

Maybe it's a trick, and he wants to trap me. I'm going to the temple to do important God stuff.

No matter the reason these smart, rich, busy, successful, religious people talked themselves out of helping the guy, in doing so, they took themselves out of the equation to do something that could have really made a difference for someone who was hurting.

Stay Alert

You have to be careful to notice the opportunities to serve when they come your way. If you aren't, you can easily miss out on doing something great for God and for another person. Sure, I get it, you're busy, and you're pursuing big things at work or school. Plus, the kids have soccer, baseball, and basketball practice. But there are needs outside your routine that need your specific attention. Someone in your sphere of influence needs you to collide with their circumstances. Don't look the other way, and don't talk yourself out of your next opportunity to do something great.

You might be saying to yourself right now, "That's easier said than done." Well, you're right, serving isn't easy. But here are a few things to consider for some of the most common excuses I've heard for not serving.

Excuse 1: They Don't Want Help from an Outsider

When you find someone who needs your help, look past the differences that separate the two of you, whether they are religious, social, racial, or economical. Helping people who are different from you is going to expand your world-view and give you an opportunity to take Christ into worlds where you may not feel totally comfortable.

Excuse 2: I Need All the Tax Deductions I Can Get, and Helping Them Is Not a Write-Off

You're right! In most cases you are not going to get any economic advantage for extending Christ's mercy to those in need. But you will reap untold eternal benefits for doing so. "Store up for yourselves treasures in heaven, where moths and vermin do not destroy, and where thieves do not break in and steal" (Matt. 6:20 NIV).

Excuse 3: I'll Never Solve All Their Problems, So Why Even Try?

Serving someone who has a need does not mean they have become a lifelong project for you. How deep you decide to dive into helping someone is entirely up to you. But in most cases your work will entail pulling them out of their immediate need and calling it a day. If they need more help, it's usually a good idea to get others involved in the serving process.

Excuse 4: If I Help Them Now, They'll Never Leave Me Alone

Your role is not to be a person's savior. That's Jesus' job. Your job is to help meet immediate needs and, if need be, point them in the right direction for long-term help. Most people who need a hand will just be glad you sacrificed twenty minutes and a few dollars to help them out of a bind.

Here's the deal: if we're not careful, we'll become a brilliant defense attorney in our mind, and we'll come up with all sorts of great-sounding reasons not to help people in need. Every time we do that, we're stealing significance from our own lives.

Excuse 5: I Can't Afford to Help Anyone

In most circumstances you will not need to reach for your wallet to help someone. A kind word, a caring act such as checking in on someone, and visiting someone in the hospital are all free to do.

But let's be real, serving people will always cost you something whether it's time, money, or energy. Every time you help someone, it's a worthy pursuit. Greatness doesn't come cheap. In fact, I'd argue that greatness can be bought.

Greatness Can Be Bought

Any great adventure you go on will require you to pay a price. I believe that price is money, time, and energy. Jesus calls it "counting the costs." And as you begin to serve others, you're going to have to decide now if you're willing to pay the price.

> "Suppose one of you wants to build a tower. Won't you first sit down and estimate the cost to see if you have enough money to complete it?" (Luke 14:28 NIV)

Jesus is talking about the difference between good intentions and life-changing actions. He's asking His listeners if they intend to serve people or just talk about it. He's asking them if they're serious about serving others, if they've really counted the costs to do so.

Here are a few questions you need to answer that will help you count the costs of helping others:

- Are you willing to fight mind games and help people in need in your sphere of influence?
- Are you willing to allow your schedule to be interrupted to help others?
- Are you willing to sacrifice some of your family's entertainment budget so someone else's life can be better?

- Are you willing to go out of your way, putting your goals on hold, so you can help someone?

This is what Jesus means when He tells us to count the costs. For me, counting the costs can circle back to the proud funeral I hope to one day have. Do I want to go out with as many dollars and material things as possible, or do I want to go out with a bunch of stories of life-change?

If we're willing to spend time, energy, and resources to serve others, then greatness can be bought!

Chapter 15

McMuffins Change Lives

Though serving can be costly, it can take you swiftly toward a life of greatness, purpose, and meaning and into a real relationship with our Creator. Serving takes you toward greatness in the eyes of the people you love and sets the stage for a funeral you'll be proud of someday.

Serving takes you away from things like self-pity and depression and toward things like joy and satisfaction. "Whoever refreshes others will be refreshed" (Prov. 11:25 NIV). Serving takes you closer to God!

> Dear children, let us not love with words or speech but with actions and in truth. This is how we know that we belong to the truth and how we set our hearts at rest in his presence. (1 John 3:18–19 NIV)

Serving is how we put our faith into action, and it allows us to experience the presence of God. That's why God wants each of us to find someone to serve. At the end of the day, it changes that person's life, it changes your life, and you'll be closer to God. I've watched this concept play out in the life of a good friend of mine named Scott.

Scott is one of those guys you just don't like because he is good at everything! A good-looking guy, best amateur jump shot in town, smart, successful, beautiful girlfriend, and always smiling. You know the guy I'm writing about because you just pictured someone from high school and got frustrated thinking of him and all the mountains he's conquered!

Six years ago Scott was a successful businessman who owned his own Internet business, had real-estate deals going on the side, and was thinking about proposing to the woman of his dreams. By all accounts life was perfect. But then out of nowhere his perfect life began to unravel. First, his lucrative business tanked. Then all of his real-estate ventures went south. And as the bloodletting encompassed several months, he took on a massive debt load. Then to throw salt in the wound, he went through a painful breakup with his girlfriend.

In less than a year Scott went from the best financial shape of his life and deeply in love to the worst financial situation he could have imagined, alone, depressed, and heartbroken. By the time he reached out to me, he was at the end of his rope. Scott confided in me that he was so tired of hurting, questioning, and worrying that he didn't even want to live anymore. He said he actually prayed daily that God would end his life.

At one time or another, all of us will endure pain, but when our spirit gets crushed and we loose all hope, life can seem unbearable. Scott felt that death would be the only relief he'd get.

Desperate for change, Scott started attending our downtown Denver Red Rocks Church campus. To avoid an extra hour of depressing alone time at home, he started going early to church and helping set up for Sunday morning services.

After helping set up one Sunday morning, Scott and a few guys headed down the street to McDonalds to grab some breakfast. As they walked out of the restaurant, Scott saw a homeless man on the street. Feeling bad for the man, Scott handed him his Egg McMuffin. The man was thankful for what Scott had done.

Scott didn't think much about it until he felt some hunger pains as he walked back to the church. As he neared the church, he also noticed that his long-held sadness and depression had suddenly lifted. If only for a few minutes, Scott felt good about himself. The next week Scott went to church early, helped set up, then headed to McDonalds. On his way back to the church he passed out a couple of Egg McMuffins to homeless people and invited them to church. This became a weekly ritual for Scott and one of his favorite things to do.

Incredibly, some of Scott's new friends came to church and allowed God to change their lives. Our staff noticed that God was changing Scott's life, but more important, so did Scott. Looking back now, he says God used those experiences to show him that he had a gift for helping those in need. He also felt that God was calling him to do similar work seven days a week.

Scott and I talked, and he told me he wanted to connect his love of sports with his desire to help people in need. The problem was, he had no idea what such a career would look like. Fortunately, I did. For years I'd wanted a sports ministry at our church so people could hang out, play, and form the kind of relationships we talked about in the Relationship section—you know, the kind that can take people closer to God.

Under Scott's direction, four years ago we started a sports league. We started with one basketball team comprised of eight guys. Today we have more than two thousand people playing in our sports leagues. Scott, as a full-time employee, runs the entire thing!

One of the coolest elements of the league has nothing to do with sports. Each season teams take a week off to serve the greater Denver community. Our soccer team brings in Down syndrome children and plays soccer with them; our climbing group takes a portable climbing wall to an inner-city school and teaches kids how to climb; our football teams hold football camps for kids from the Adoption Exchange; our basketball teams do eight-week camps for orphans and foster children. These are just some of the examples of serving that our teams do.

Recently our entire league collaborated to fill two semi-trailers full of clothes and food for a ministry that will now be able to feed and clothe homeless individuals in downtown Denver twice a day for the next year! Thousands of lives will be changed this year through serving others because of a sports program run by a once-suicidal guy named Scott who had nothing but an Egg McMuffin and a desire to help people in need.

I talked to Scott recently and asked him how his life had changed because of serving others.

"Shawn, I'm the happiest I've ever been, and my life is a thousand times better than I ever thought possible," he said, noting he met his dream girl and married her. He couldn't be more in love with their new baby, and he absolutely loves serving people today more than he ever loved making money. "To think, it all started with an Egg McMuffin!"

This is the kind of story God wants for you too! You and I don't know exactly what God will do through us when we start serving. We can't know exactly who will be affected and how it will all turn out. But you should know now that when you are willing to spend your time, energy, and resources in serving other people, God promises to:

- Change people's lives
- Change your life
- Change how you'll be remembered

Serving is a vehicle you simply can't afford not to use! As Jesus once said to His buddies, "Now go and do the same."

Vehicle 5

Giving

Chapter 16

Show Me the Money

how me the money!" is a phrase you'll never forget if
you saw the movie *Jerry McGuire*. Tom Cruise yelled
that phrase over and over while sitting at his high-
falutin sports agency desk. It was funny then, but when I
heard a pastor say it for the first time, I wasn't laughing. In
fact, I was furious. I hadn't had the kind of week where I
wanted to hear somebody at church asking me for money
and especially not the pastor!

Jill and I were newly married, and I was interning at a
church for $50 a week, studying to become a pastor. Jill was
raking in the cash too as a sixth-grade teacher at a Christian
school. Our salaries combined added up to just about nothing. We were as poor as either of us had ever been in our
lives. I'm talking, crying when the gas bill comes kind of
poor. We didn't eat out, we didn't buy clothes, and we didn't

even dream of going on a vacation. We bought groceries, paid our student loans and rent, and then prayed we had enough money left to fill up the gas tank in our car.

On a Wednesday night a friend invited us to a restaurant in downtown Chicago for a surprise party for her husband. There was no way we could afford something like that, but we felt we couldn't say no because they were such good friends. Later that night at dinner, as I was eating my salad, the cheapest thing on the menu, I watched my friend opening presents from his wife and coworkers. He finally got the elaborate wrapping off of a giant box and pulled a gigantic sombrero out for everyone to see. Attached to it was note: "Jer, enjoy a fun-filled, all-expenses-paid vacation in sunny Mexico!"

I about spit out my food! He just pulled up in a car that's worth more than my entire net worth and now he's going to Mexico for a week—for free! I was crushed. Life wasn't fair. As I was processing the realization that his life was better than mine would ever be, everyone started clapping around the table. I reluctantly joined in while thinking, *Mexico, huh? I hope you choke on a burrito and drown.*

I was being petty and pathetic. But life, as finances were concerned, was not allowing me to celebrate our friend's good fortune. Two nights later I came home from work, walked in the back door of our apartment, and was met by my wife wearing a sundress with a mischievous look on her face.

"What's going on?"

There was no way we were going out for dinner again, and she was far too overdressed to watch the Lakers game with me on the couch. As I tried to figure out what was up, she took my coat, laid it on the table, and escorted me into our tiny dining room. What I saw floored me. There was a plate of tacos sitting on a side table, with nachos and salsa. Our little radio was in the corner of the room with an ocean sound track playing. She had moved our tiny table out of the room and replaced it with two beach towels on the floor lying next to each other. There was a lamp above the towels, with yellow construction paper around the top, making it look like a child's version of the sun. She held my hand and looked me in the eyes and said, "Relax honey, tonight we're going to Mexico."

I couldn't help but cry as I hugged my wife and realized one more time that I married the coolest chick in the entire world! That night we ate dinner on the floor and lay on our beach towels and talked about life.

Sunday rolled around and we went to church, the same church building where we first met and both worked at during the week. The pastor got up and told a funny story about his trip the week before in Hawaii and then said, "OK church, let's receive the tithes and offering today." He read some verse about being generous and followed it up with, "Now let's give big today!"

I wanted to throw my phone at him! "Let's give big today? Are you serious?"

I kept rolling his words over and over in my mind: "Give big." What nerve he had! I've seen his big house and his wife's shiny new car. He just got back from two weeks in Hawaii. Give big? I just went to Mexico . . . in my living room!

An anger I hadn't ever known consumed me. And for the first time in my life, I couldn't figure out why this man, or God for that matter, could possibly want my money. I barely had any!

You might know exactly what I'm talking about. You've been there, scraping just to get by, praying for a financial miracle and wishing you could hit fast-forward on life just so you can get to the next payday.

If that's you, I understand. I also know that when you saw those six magic letters that spell *Giving* you were tempted to skip this chapter. I'm glad you didn't because this vehicle is so powerful and life-changing, yet also possibly more misunderstood than anything we've examined so far.

You see, giving for many people is by far the most difficult spiritual vehicle to operate. It's difficult because it's your money, right? We work hard for it. We usually don't feel like we have enough of it, and why in the world would God want it anyway? If you've already been asking these questions, I get it. I've been there.

But giving is absolutely necessary as you move closer to God. So, in order for you even to begin to think about using the vehicle of giving, you're going to need a big-picture perspective that will reveal God's point of view on giving.

It's All from Him

First of all, God reminds us that whatever money we have, whatever we do possess, whether it's a shopping cart full of clothes or a mansion full of antiques, it's all from Him. Everything you and I possess is the result of God's giving it to us. He put it like this: "You may say to yourself, 'My power and the strength of my hands have produced this wealth for me.' But remember the LORD your God, for it is he who gives you the ability to produce wealth, and so confirms his covenant, which he swore to your ancestors, as it is today" (Deut. 8:17–18 NIV).

God knows how we are. He knows we take credit for everything we have. We pat ourselves on the back for the work ethic that produced our money. Our skills, our brains, our initiative, and our ability to take risks. Yep, we take credit for those too. We find all sorts of reasons to convince ourselves that we deserve all of our stuff because, after all, we earned it. God says, "get real." "Remember the LORD your God, for it is he who gives you the ability to produce wealth."

I was reminded of this truth on a trip to South Africa in a place called Freedom Park. Thousands of people there live in houses made out of trash. Freedom Park has no food or clean drinking water. Once a week somebody brings residents a bag of grain, and a rusty trailer brings in dirty pond water for drinking, but that's about it. Almost everybody there has HIV. I met a three-year-old child walking around the field calling for his mommy and daddy, not realizing both of his parents had died from the same HIV virus that he had had since birth.

Now imagine if you'd been born in Freedom Park with HIV and at age three both of your parents died, leaving you on the ground next to a hut made of trash. Think how you would feel knowing that the disease you were born with imprisoned you so that you would never leave the field. And because of your lack of medical care, your life was going to be cut short.

Unless you are currently reading this book from Freedom Park, that's probably not the situation you were born into. Why not? Did you deserve your parents more than an infant born in South Africa? Did your work ethic allow you to be born without HIV more so than a child in Freedom Park? No. No!

You were born where you were born, in the country where you were born, to the parents you gave you birth or adopted you, with the mind and talents you were born with; and you did nothing to earn or deserve any of it. Every opportunity for an abundance of food, education, earning, shelter, and access to health care and clean water is the direct result of God! You had nothing to do with it. God says He will help you and me use the vehicle of giving if we first can be realistic about the fact that everything we have comes directly from Him.

If we can wrap our minds around that fact, then we can begin to understand that to God giving is really just returning to Him a small portion of what He gave us in the first place. And for reasons we will get to shortly, God does expect us to return some of our resources to Him.

> But since you excel in everything—in faith, in speech, in knowledge, in complete earnestness and in the love we have kindled in you—see that you also excel in this grace of giving. (2 Cor. 8:7 NIV)

God says that just as you should excel in regular prayer, studying of the Word, and relationships, you should also make sure you excel in the area of giving. This vehicle may be tough to get moving, but once you do it, it will take you closer to God faster than you ever imagined! Read that last sentence one more time. No, for real, reread it. That still may be a confusing concept for you, but it's true. So, how can giving your money to God bring you closer to Him?

That's the question I wrestled with as I sat in church listening to the pastor talk about giving big. At that point in my life, I simply couldn't land on an answer when it came to why I should give my money to God. But I was determined to find an answer.

Chapter 17

Why Give?

I spent years trying to figure out how giving could possibly affect my relationship with God. And it just never made sense to me until I read Matthew 6:21, "For where your treasure is, there your heart will be also."

Jesus was answering this same question for His best friends when He first said it, and it's still true today some two thousand years later. This verse simply reminds us that wherever our money goes, our heart will follow. Here's the deal: God doesn't want my money; He wants my heart. Years later I realized God doesn't need my money or need my heart. The truth is, I need Him to have my heart.

Jesus said, "I have come so that they may have life and have it in abundance" (John 10:10). The abundant life He wants for us comes only when our heart is fully connected with God. The life I dream of—the life God has in store for me—becomes more and more of a reality the closer I get to the Father. The same goes for you today, which you already know in part since you are reading this book about getting closer to God.

God doesn't need your heart; you need Him to have your heart. Wherever your money goes, your heart will follow. If you don't believe me, run a little test on yourself. Visit your broker and invest your life savings into United Airlines stock. I guarantee your interest in United will soar higher than their planes. You'll be sitting in the doctor's office looking for magazines with airplanes on the cover. You'll be checking stocks and watching trends. You'll talk about the airline industry with friends and even find yourself praying for United Airlines to succeed. Why the sudden change of heart? Because *where your treasure is, there your heart will be also.*

As crazy as it might sound, giving truly takes us closer to God faster than we might have ever realized. This is a lesson I learned shortly after my fake living-room vacation to Mexico.

The same Sunday the pastor asked the congregation to give big, Jill and I sat in our driveway after church talking about money, our bills, and how we'd squeak by until the next paycheck. But Jill flipped the conversation upside down when she said something startling: "Let's just give it all away!"

"Give all what away?" I asked. "We don't have anything to give."

"I'm serious, let's just give it all to God because I'm tired of worrying about what little money we do have."

My wife is a better person than I am.

"Well, how much do we have right now if we added it all up?"

Jill flipped through her wallet, ran a couple of quick calculations, then proclaimed almost proudly, "Pretty close to fifty dollars!"

"Fifty!" I blurted out, not sure why a twenty-seven-year-old man of my stature would only have fifty dollars to his name. I stared at Jill as if to say, go ahead make my day.

"It's a start," she said.

"OK, let's do this," I said bravely. "Let's give big. Ha!"

Jill whipped out her checkbook and wrote a check for fifty dollars to a ministry we both believed in.

"I'll mail it tomorrow," she said.

Right there we held hands and prayed, "God, our finances are more than we know what to do with right now, so from now on our finances are YOUR problem."

Somewhat stunned, we went inside and didn't talk to each other for an hour or so. Two days later while I was at church, a man in a three-piece suit approached me. As he got closer, I realized his suit was amazing, and his eyes were locked on me.

"Can I help you?" I asked, somewhat intimidated.

He just handed me an envelope that had my name on the outside and said, "God woke me up in the middle of the night and told me to give this to you."

"OK," I said as he turned on his heel and walked away.

I stared at the envelope and immediately began to wonder if it was a death threat or if my past had caught up with me and I had been served. Not wanting to let anyone know I was scared, I walked out of the church and to my car. There I sat in the driver's seat and opened the envelope. Inside was a check for $5,000.

Tears fell from my eyes. I'd been a Christian for more than two years and had never felt as close to God as I did in that moment. I remember looking up to heaven and saying, "You are paying attention. You are with me." God was listening to my prayers and honoring our obedience to give big and let Him be in charge of our finances. The check in my hand felt like a direct message from God, and He was screaming to me, letting me know He was paying attention to my needs.

Giving had taken me closer to God than I'd ever been before, and God wants this same closeness with you. But how can you jump-start this vehicle?

Chapter 18

How to Give

Martin Luther said, "There are three conversions a person needs to experience: the conversion of the head, the conversion of the heart, and the conversion of the pocketbook."

When Jill and I gave God our last $50 was the first time in our married life that we really trusted God with our finances. Because of it, I couldn't believe how much God was doing in my life. I had truly had a conversion of the pocketbook, which meant my heart had followed my money toward God, and I loved it.

Let's say you're suddenly inspired and want to embrace this idea of giving. If so, where should you start? Will $50 suffice? Or do you need to empty your checking account? Maybe. But probably not. These questions and more I'll answer in a crash course I call "Giving God's Way."

In Malachi God has an insightful conversation concerning the Nation of Israel: "'I the LORD do not change. So you, O descendants of Jacob, are not destroyed. Ever since the time of your forefathers you have turned away from my decrees and have not kept them. Return to me, and I will return to you,' says the LORD Almighty. But you ask, 'How are we to return?'" (Mal. 3:6–7 NIV).

Notice that this is not a conversation about money; it's about people being closer to God. Something is going on that has caused Israel to be distant from God, and He is about to tell them exactly how to move closer back to Him.

> "Ever since the time of your forefathers you have turned away from my decrees and have not kept them. Return to me, and I will return to you," says the LORD Almighty.
>
> But you ask: "How can we return?"
>
> "Will a man rob God? Yet you rob me."
>
> But you ask: "How do we rob you?"
>
> "In tithes and offerings. You are under a curse— the whole nation of you—because you are robbing me. Bring the whole tithe into the storehouse, that there may be food in my house. Test me in this," says the LORD Almighty. (Mal. 3:7–10 NIV)

God says, "Because you are not giving the way I've instructed, you are separated from Me, and now you are suffering because of it." In other words, their treasure wasn't going to God, so neither were their hearts, and that was negatively affecting every other area of their lives. The good news for the Israelites is that they do realize that they want to be closer to God, so they ask Him how they can return to Him.

God keeps His answer simple, direct, and succinct when He tells them that if they want to be closer to Him, it will start with their "tithes and offerings." That word *tithe* means 10 percent of one's income, and "offerings" refer to any amount above and beyond the 10 percent.

God explains that not only will the church be taken care of when they give this way, but they will also receive blessings in ways they won't even be able to handle. If I were writing that, I'd put it this way: Give God the first 10 percent of your income, be willing to give even more away if God calls you to do so, and you will receive some crazy blessings and move closer to God than you ever imagined.

But God doesn't stop there. He wants the Israelites— and us—to know that His words are not empty. So He implores the Israelites to test Him so that He can blow their minds with His blessing on their lives.

You may have heard that since this portion of Scripture is from the Old Testament, it's not as relevant to our lives today. God is so serious about us giving to Him on a regular basis that He asks us to test Him. We also need to remember that in the New Testament Jesus didn't do away with this idea of giving 10 percent of our income and offerings. In fact, He takes giving to a whole new level in Matthew when He says there may be times when He asks His followers to give it all to God (Matt. 19:16–26).

What's way more important than arguing over a specific percentage is just starting. I personally can't read the Scriptures and justify giving God less than 10 percent of my income. I challenge you to read the Scriptures and ask God with an open heart what percentage you should start giving back to Him. Start there and simply be willing to allow God to guide you into the future concerning your giving.

Four Easy Steps to Giving

To help you get started, here are four basic steps I adhere to that make giving as easy as possible:

1. Preplan
2. Pick a percentage to give to your local church
3. Set aside that percentage before anything else
4. Be consistent

Look at what the apostle Paul says to Christ followers concerning giving to their local church: "Now about the collection for God's people: Do what I told the Galatian churches to do. On the first day of every week, each one of you should set aside a sum of money in keeping with his income, saving it up, so that when I come no collections will have to be made" (1 Cor. 16:1–2 NIV).

Let's dissect this verse into four easy steps for giving God's way.

On the first day of every week:

1. Preplan

Notice the text says, "On the first day of every week, each one of you should set aside a sum of money" (1 Cor. 16:2 NIV). Before you get behind the wheel of giving, you need to nail down the minimum amount you are going to bring to God on a regular basis. You need to "set aside a sum of money." This is the opposite of just winging it on Sunday mornings, deciding how you feel, and/or pulling out whatever bills happen to be in your purse or wallet. Giving should not be a game-time decision. Know what you are giving each time you give. Preplan your giving.

2. Pick a Percentage

Paul says your giving should be in keeping with your income. The way you and I can give in keeping with our income is by picking and sticking to a percent that we'll give back to God on a regular basis. Think of it like this: if you make a little, 10 percent is little. If you make a lot, 10 percent will be a lot. By fixing the percent to begin with, the amount you give will stay the same in relation to what you make, which allows you to give "in keeping with your income" (1 Cor. 16:2 NIV).

3. Set Aside Your Giving First

Paul says, "On the *first day* of every week." The day of the week you give is not critical to giving the way God wants you to give. The point God is making is that the first 10 percent of our income should come off the top and be reserved for Him. This is as practical as it gets. I don't know about you, but if I pay all my bills, spend the rest on whatever I want, then get to the end of the week and see what's left to give God, there isn't much there. So we set aside that percentage of our income for God before we spend money on anything else.

4. Be Consistent

"On the first day of *every* week." We shouldn't fall into the trap of only giving to God sometimes. We need to give to God at all times including good times, bad times, lean times, and times of plenty. Give to God all the time! I have found—and you will too—that God can do more with our 90 percent than we can do with 100 percent. He will provide for you! But don't hold back; be consistent. And He promises to bless you in ways that you won't even have room enough to store it.

Our consistency in giving God's way is preceded by some pretty big statements:

> "Bring the whole tithe into the storehouse, that there may be food in my house. Test me in this," says the LORD Almighty, "and see if I will not throw open the floodgates of heaven and pour out so much blessing that you will not have room enough for it." (Mal. 3:10 NIV)

> "Give, and it will be given to you. A good measure, pressed down, shaken together and running over, will be poured into your lap. For with the measure you use, it will be measured to you." (Luke 6:38 NIV)

> One man gives freely, yet gains even more; another withholds unduly, but comes to poverty. A generous man will prosper; he who refreshes others will himself be refreshed. (Prov. 11:24–25 NIV)

Giving When It Hurts

When we obey and are generous, especially in the middle of difficult financial times, God is free to do some of the biggest miracles we'll ever see. Over the years I've seen that giving under duress takes us closer to God than almost anything I've ever experienced.

Eight years ago Jill and I moved from Rockford to Denver, Colorado, to be a part of starting Red Rocks Church. Like any start-up company, money was tight. The staff was small, and we were living month to month. By "tight" I mean no real paychecks, no health insurance, and no job security.

Not long after we started the church, a missionary from Ethiopia asked us if we could help him buy a van for his ministry. We talked and prayed about it, and everyone on our team agreed we should buy it for him. It was $10,000, which was about $9,000 more than we'd ever spent on anything and would completely deplete our savings, but we felt like we were trusting God, and surely we couldn't go wrong, right?

The next day Scott Bruegman, my good friend and one of the original founders of Red Rocks Church, who was also handling the finances at the time, approached me with an atypical serious look on his face.

"We gotta talk," he said. "We're almost out of money."

Todd, also a friend and one of the original founders of the church, reported that to add to our financial woes the fire marshal had paid us a visit and informed us that we needed to spend thousands of dollars to get part of the church up to code, and until we did that, we could no longer have church there. Scott went on to tell me that we didn't have enough money to pay rent, and the small stipend the staff counted on wasn't there either.

I rounded up our team, and we had a heart-to-heart talk. Questions filled the room. *Is this the day the dream is over?* I'm not sure. *Had we done everything we could to keep this church open?* I think so. *What about the $10,000 we earmarked for the missionary in Ethiopia, did we send him the check yet?* Boom! There was our answer.

"Let's call the guy, explain the situation, and tell him it's either his van or this church is going under," was my first thought. "We have to look at the bigger picture here. Save the church, and we'll help the missionary when we are back on our feet." That's what made the most sense.

We just sat there and started praying. Afterwards, we all just sat there staring at one another. It was as if no one wanted to be the first to speak. We all knew we were at a crossroads and had to make one of two choices: keep the money for ourselves and do what made sense or go through with what we thought God was calling us to do and give the money away.

"Let's give him the van!" one of the guys said.

After a long, uncomfortable pause . . . , "Yeah, let's do it," somebody else said.

Everybody started shaking heads in agreement. One guy jumped out of his seat, then another, and another. We started high-fiving one another and chest bumping. "Let's do this!" someone shouted. It was like we'd just gotten a halftime pep talk and we were ready to go back out on the field and take care of business!

"Give it all!"

"God's got our back!"

"That's right, let's get crazy!"

"Yeah, . . . let's do it!"

Scott waited for the adrenaline to wear off, then looked at each of us. "So just to be clear," he said, "give him all the cash, empty the account? Just want to be sure before I pull the trigger."

As crazy as it sounded, we were all in. If the church and our budding careers as church planters went down in flames, who cared? At least we went out swinging! I couldn't help but think of the times God had delivered when I was faithful during the worst of financial circumstances. I also couldn't help but think of Him asking the Israelites to test Him when it came to giving.

Even so, the practical side of me was screaming, "This is stupid!"

"Let's pray that God will open the floodgates!" someone said. "Let's ask God to take care of us in ways we can't possibly take care of ourselves."

The guys all nodded, and we prayed again with faith, expectancy, and if we were honest—fear.

As I drove home that night, I couldn't believe what we had just done. How am I going to tell Jill we failed and that we moved our family to Denver for nothing? What will I write in the e-mail to the people in the church to let them know the church was finished? I was scared to death but also excited about taking a God risk even though it was a high-risk venture filled with uncertainties.

The next morning I got a call from a pastor friend. I hadn't talked to him in more than a year.

"Hello," I said into the earpiece.

"Shawn, it's Kevin Kringel," he said. "I was praying this morning, and God just put it on my heart for our church to send Red Rocks a check. Do you guys need any money?"

I couldn't even speak as my lip quivered and tears fell from my eyes. I was such a sissy, but I couldn't control it.

"You have no idea what an answer to prayer this call is, man," I stammered. "I'll call you back in a few minutes."

Like a schoolgirl I balled my eyes out. I couldn't let him know, I was breaking all man laws.

Just like sitting in my car a few years before, I found myself looking up again and saying, "God, You are watching! You are with me!"

A few days later we got a check for more than eight thousand dollars from my friend's church. And almost to the dollar, it paid all our bills, the rent, and the stipends for the staff. And we were able to open the doors for service that next Sunday! It was a great reminder that as followers of Christ it is simply impossible to outgive God.

At that moment I hadn't felt so connected with God in a long time. One act of obedience with our money, and all of a sudden it felt like God and I were sharing a cubicle at work, and we were doing life together again.

Here's the bottom line: operating the giving vehicle will be scary at first, but the benefits are through the roof. Regardless of your fears and regardless of how counterintuitive this may be for you, you can give, and it really will change everything about your life!

Vehicle 6

Sharing

Chapter 19

Scared to Death

She was seventeen years old when she had sex for the first time. She was a junior in high school. She knew better, but he said he loved her, and she wanted to be loved so badly that she was willing to do whatever it took to make him happy. A couple months later it was confirmed: she was pregnant and scared to death. She was sick with fear when she imagined telling her parents and friends. But even worse was the thought that she would soon be a mother. After all, she was just a kid about to have a kid.

She and the boy decided to fess up. They went together to tell her parents the news and feel their wrath. Shortly after doing so, the boy dropped out of sight. He wouldn't answer her calls, and when she went by his house, he was never home. No one knew where he had gone or how long he'd be gone. She heard from a friend of a friend that he had fled town, never to return.

After fighting off the notion of abortion more times than she'd like to admit, she gave birth to a son. She was a lonely, scared, high school girl trying to learn to be a mother on her own. Not knowing how to cope with life, and spending time with the wrong people, she began experimenting with drugs. It brought the temporary relief and escape she needed, but her addiction quickly consumed her like a wildfire on a parched hillside. Before she knew it, she was a heroine addict with a two-year-old son. A son that she had no clue what to do with and was barely sober enough to care for. Her mistakes and errors in judgment were compounded when she married her drug dealer. He couldn't fill the void in her soul so she began having an affair with his best friend. Maybe he held the magic formula that could bring her out of her tailspin.

She soon found out he couldn't. Life became more than she could handle so she did the unthinkable. She strapped her son in a car seat and left him on the porch of a stranger's house with a note attached.

She didn't know it then because she was completely hopeless, but all she needed was Jesus. He could've helped her. He could've given her the peace that seemed so elusive. He could have wrapped His arms of grace and love around her and given her the hope she so desperately needed. But she didn't know such things existed so she kissed her son good-bye, then she made her way to a nearby freeway overpass and jumped.

"In his name the nations will put their hope." (Matt. 12:21 NIV)

Jesus Christ is the hope of this world, and if you've never put your faith in Him and allowed Him to change your life from the inside out, there's no better time than right now! As people all around the globe will tell you, Jesus really is the source of hope for our lives today. When we come in contact with the truth that God loves us so much that He allowed His Son to die for us, and all we have to do is call out to Jesus, ask Him to forgive us of our sins, and put our trust in Him, we're saved, we're forgiven, and we're on a road toward a life with authentic hope here and now and heaven forever.

It's a shame that nobody told the girl about this hope before she jumped off of the bridge. But when people don't share what they know about God, lives that could have been altered aren't. It's a sad but extremely simple equation. When people don't share the good news of Jesus, people perish.

Spiritual vehicle 5 is all about sharing our faith with hurting and lost people. Oftentimes I've wondered how the girl's life might have been different if someone had reached out to her with the message of Jesus Christ before she jumped. I know that's a heavy way to start this section, but what we're talking about here is real, and real lives and real deaths are at stake. We live in a real world where people are really hurting and really hopeless, and we have the opportunity through *sharing* to bring them hope in a way that will change everything in their lives and guarantee eternity in heaven.

We live in a hurting and broken world, and we have all been hurting and broken. Although unpleasant to think about, we are all just coming out of trouble, we are in trouble, or we are headed for trouble. Jesus told us all along that we should expect that: "I have told you these things, so that in me you may have peace. In the world you will have trouble. But take heart! I have overcome the world" (John 16:33 NIV).

Jesus reminds us of the troubles we will face and encourages us in the fact that when He is in our lives, we can overcome it all. We can endure, overcome, and persevere through things we never could on our own; and because of our connection to Him, we can live with hope now and forever in heaven. This is an amazing reality for every person who commits his or her life to Jesus. That's why it's absolutely crucial that we share this good news with everyone who comes into our sphere of influence.

We share it because this world needs it. Even people who seem happy, healthy, and successful desperately need a relationship with Jesus Christ. As best-selling author Rick Warren wrote in *The Purpose Driven Life*: "We must remember that everybody needs Jesus, no matter how contented or successful they appear to be. Without Christ, they are hopelessly lost and headed for eternal separation from God."[4]

This world desperately needs the hope we have found in Jesus. As discussed earlier in this book, there is only one way to heaven. Jesus is that way, and just as we need to receive salvation from Him, so do the people in our world. As we'll see in this section, He expects you and me to play a part in that. Now I don't know about you, but sometimes that scares me!

I told you in the previous section that after moving to Rockford I got involved in a small group. Little did I know at the time, but that small-group experience would change my life. I got the opportunity to lead the group from time to time, tell my personal story, and help others. I loved it. I decided that I wanted to continue doing that for the rest of my life, but I had no clue what that meant. *How many ex-drug users do church work?*, I thought. I knew then, as crazy as it sounded, I wanted to be in some type of full-time ministry. And wouldn't you know it, that same youth pastor, Jeanne, the one who told me to leave Hollywood, talked to me about doing a two-year internship that would prepare me to be a pastor. *What? Do you know me?*

I laughed just thinking about it, and to my own surprise, I agreed, still having no real idea what I was getting myself into. It's crazy how God will begin to change the direction of your life when you really put Him in the driver's seat. My life was so turned around. I went from the drug culture to training for pastoral work. On many levels it didn't make any sense.

By operating the spiritual vehicles laid out for you in this book, you are already putting Him in the driver's seat of your life. He may fast-track you in the same direction you're headed now. He may put you on a path you may never have dreamed of, but know this: when you put God in full control of your life, He'll amaze you with new destinations!

An amazing moment for me came in the form of the senior pastor at the church where I was interning asking me to speak for a few minutes during part of a Sunday church service. I was scared to death, doubtful if I was up to such a task, and suddenly doubtful if being a pastor was what I really wanted to do with my life.

I knew enough to know that I knew little about the Bible, and I was deathly afraid to stand up in front of people and talk. I had vowed I would never do that. And now the boss was demanding that I do just that. I remember my message almost word for word that day. I told people that God loves us so we should love others. It was simple, honest, and from my heart. But it wasn't particularly well crafted or even delivered in a compelling way. By all accounts it was more of an act of obedience than a sermon to be remembered.

On the way home from that traumatic experience, I was talking to Chad, my buddy who was also interning at the church and currently living with me and my new wife. We hit a four-way stop, and the car across from us started to go at the wrong time. As we all know, the rules of a four-way stop are elementary. Since I stopped first, I'd go first. So I started to go and so did the driver of the car who was there second. We met in the middle, our cars inches from each other. Like men do, we just stared at each other. This was a Wild West showdown in the middle of Rockford, Illinois.

Suddenly he put both hands in the air as if to say, "What's up man!" I put my hands in the air and asked him the same thing. We were talking to each other through our windshields as we gave each other the "mall stare." Then the tension rose when he rolled down his window and flipped me the bird. I'm a pastor/intern, a man of the cloth, so what did I do? Well, I rolled my window down and flipped him off with even more enthusiasm and passion than he did. This prompted him to get out of his car, so I followed suit. I started walking toward him and Chad yelled, "Johnson!"

"Not now!" I replied, still in fighting stance. "It's go time."

"Johnson!"

"What?" I asked with great irritation.

"You preached about the love of God eight minutes ago!"

Stunned by his reminder, I paused and, just like Tommy Boy, said, "Oh, yeah!"

Not wanting to lose face, I looked back at the driver who was now poised to fight. With as much controlled anger as I could muster, I slowly pointed at him and sternly said, "I would love it if you . . . went first sir."

Like a puppy with his tail between his legs, I got back into my car and drove home.

As I pulled into the driveway, I decided that day that I'd never talk to anyone about God again because I was just not worthy! I had all kinds of problems, dysfunctions, and faults. When it came to talking about God, from that point on, I'd leave that to the experts.

You ever feel that way? You've heard either directly or through the grapevine that, as a follower of Jesus Christ, you're supposed to tell other people about Him, and the mere notion of doing so freaks you out. You know you, and you know all the problems with you, and you are certain you are not the person who ought to be out evangelizing about the Son of God. If so, you're in good company: most people have similar feelings at one time or another.

The problem for us is that Jesus never asked us if we were comfortable with the idea. He didn't suggest that we do this and then leave it up to us to decide, He demands it.

Listen to what Jesus said to some of His disciples the first time He ever talked to them: "As He was walking along the Sea of Galilee, He saw two brothers, Simon, who was called Peter, and his brother Andrew. They were casting a net into the sea, since they were fishermen. 'Follow Me,' He told them, 'and I will make you fish for people!'" (Matt. 4:18–19).

Jesus was telling these guys what would happen if they chose to follow Him. And if you think about it, He could have told them a lot of different things. He could have said, "If you follow Me, you'll be more disciplined or spiritual, have more biblical knowledge, and learn the secrets of the kingdom of heaven." He could have promised them all sorts of godly sounding things, but He didn't. He said, "If you want to be a follower of Mine, you're going to reach out to lost people with the message of Jesus Christ." Period! It was the first thing He ever told these guys, and just to make sure they got it, it was also the last thing He said to them. After Jesus was crucified, rose from the dead, and spent forty days walking and talking with many people, in front of five hundred eyewitnesses, including His disciples, just before He went back up into heaven, He said: "Go, therefore, and make disciples of all nations, baptizing them in the name of the Father and of the Son and of the Holy Spirit, teaching them to observe everything I have commanded you. And remember, I am with you always, to the end of the age" (Matt. 28:19–20).

As scary as it might sound, *sharing* the good news about Jesus Christ is job one for us, or at least it's supposed to be. But can we be honest for a second? Nothing about that statement makes us feel really comfortable. Many of us cringe at the idea of talking to others about God, and for many good reasons:

- I'm unworthy, unprepared, and too far from perfect.
- I didn't go to Bible school, and I'm not a theologian.
- They'll ask me questions, and I won't know the answers.
- What will they think about me if I do say something?

We get thoughts like these swirling around in our minds, and that, combined with the fact that we're really busy, will cause us never to share our faith with anyone.

Does it really matter if we do this? Are normal people like us even capable of such things? And how would this bring us closer to God? Great questions that deserve real answers, so keep reading.

Chapter 20

Lessons at the Well

Sharing our faith sounds admirable, but for most of us, it's just not something we're all that interested in doing. We get scared, we feel unworthy, we don't want to be perceived as a salesman of some sort, and we're pretty sure people we want to share it with will not want to hear it anyway.

If we do attempt to take this sharing thing out for a spin, how's that work? Where do we start? What do we do?

I thought it would be interesting if we could talk to the guys who first received these orders. The disciples, Jesus' best friends. After all, they got this news long before we did. What if we could talk to them about this sharing vehicle? *Why do we have to do this? Where do we start? And how does this bring us closer to God?* These are some of the initial questions I'd have. Let's play this out and pretend we actually get to pick their brains on this topic. What would they say?

I think for starters they'd get real passionate about the conversation. After all, they died for their desire to share the message about Christ. And I think they'd tell us that reaching out to lost people and sharing our faith is our mission as a Christ follower. I think they'd remind us that it was their mission then and our mission today. They'd get real fired up, pat us on the behind, and tell us to get out there and get in the game. And just as this pep talk would end, I'd interrupt with some huge questions. *How? What do I do? Where do I start?*

If this pretend conversation could take place, and if we could ask the disciples how to "share our faith," I think they'd start by reminding us of the last thing Jesus said before leaving this world: "Go, therefore, and make disciples of all nations, baptizing them in the name of the Father and of the Son and of the Holy Spirit" (Matt. 28:19).

Then they'd tell us the first way we share our faith is by going public with it, through baptism! Baptism is the very first thing we are commanded to do after putting our faith in Jesus Christ. And as you can see by the verse we just read, it's not a suggestion . . . it's a command! Baptism symbolizes the old you being washed away, and when you come up out of the water, it symbolizes a brand new you starting all over with Jesus as your Savior. There's something only God can explain that happens when we are baptized, something happens in the human heart that changes us. For me it solidified my new-found connection with God, and it will do the same thing for you today!

To be obedient and go public with your faith through baptism, speak with the pastor of your church and ask what steps you need to take in order to be baptized. This not only allows you to start *sharing* your faith but will also take your relationship with God to a whole new level.

For sharing our faith on an individual level, I think they'd refer back to a day their Rabbi, Jesus, taught them how to share their faith. We see this story in the Bible in the book of John, chapter 4. Let's dig into this passage for a minute and see what we can learn from it.

> So he came to a town in Samaria called Sychar, near the plot of ground Jacob had given to his son Joseph. Jacob's well was there, and Jesus, tired as he was from the journey, sat down by the well. It was about noon.
>
> When a Samaritan woman came to draw water, Jesus said to her, "Will you give me a drink?" (His disciples had gone into the town to buy food.)
>
> The Samaritan woman said to him, "You are a Jew and I am a Samaritan woman. How can you ask me for a drink?" (For Jews do not associate with Samaritans.) (John 4:5–9 NIV)

She was right, Jews didn't associate with Samaritans. In 722 BC, the Assyrians invaded Israel from the north and carried the ten northern tribes off into captivity. Historians describe the brutality of the entire ordeal. At one point the Assyrians lined up the Israelites, tied them together by putting fishhooks through the sides of their mouths, and then literally drug them away into captivity. While in captivity, some of the Assyrian men hooked up with Israeli women, and the offspring, half Jew and half Assyrian, were called Samaritans. So you see, in Jesus' time Samaritans were nothing more to the Israelites than a painful reminder of the past. And to say that Jews hated Samaritans would be an understatement. A Jew would use the word *Samaritan* as a curse word. No self-respecting Jew would be caught dead talking to a Samaritan. No self-respecting rabbi would be caught dead talking in public to a woman of any race. And so Jesus, the Rabbi, should have never been talking to a Samaritan woman in public.

If you read that entire passage, you will learn that this is not just a Samaritan woman but an unclean, outcast Samaritan woman. She'd already burned through five marriages, which in that day was unheard of, and she was currently shacking up with another guy who wasn't even her husband. She's completely despised by everyone in town. If you notice in the passage above, she was getting water at "noon." This is telling. Nobody would go get water at noon.

That was the hottest part of the day. You would get water in the morning or in the evening but never at noon unless you were trying to avoid every other person in town. I bet this woman had made the mistake of getting water when others were around and learned her lesson the hard way. When people from town saw her, they would whisper, point, and judge. This, no doubt, was more painful than she could bear.

She's unclean and shamed. And in that day they believed shame was transferable. So if you talked to an unclean person, their filth and shame would be transferred to you. We must understand that Jesus, by merely talking to this woman, was risking His entire career. You can't be full of filth and shame and be a rabbi at the same time. It just doesn't work. There's not a rabbi around who would be caught dead talking to this woman. Yet Jesus doesn't just talk to her; He gets right in the middle of her messed-up situation and starts ministering to her. He begins talking to her about God and salvation, and about that time His disciples show up on the scene.

> Just then His disciples arrived, and they were amazed that He was talking with a woman. Yet no one said, "What do You want?" or "Why are You talking with her?" (John 4:27)

To say that they were surprised is likely an understatement! I bet they were shocked, blown away, and completely confused. Jesus was breaking all of the rules; He was sham-ing Himself publicly. And not only was He jeopardizing His career; He was risking theirs as well! Then I think they'd say, "But we learned a couple things from our Rabbi that day."

1. If you really want to make a difference in the world, you'll have to take a risk on somebody that every-body else has already given up on.
2. When you do, know ahead of time, it's going to be messy.

Then I think they'd want to ask each one of us, you and me included: "Are you currently sharing your faith with anyone? Are you willing to take a risk on someone that everybody else has already given up on?"

What if we really did that today? What if we got past all of our insecurities and took a risk and shared our faith with someone that everybody else has already given up on? What if we didn't judge them like everyone else? What if we just loved them and served them, and what if God used that to change their lives for all of eternity!

That kind of partnership with God will bring a level of fulfillment that few things on this planet can. Here's the cool part: working hand-in-hand with God will also bring us closer to Him than we can possibly imagine.

I don't know why He set it up this way and why He wants to work with us on this project. To be honest, I see myself as a liability to this whole thing, but that's the way the Father wants it.

Picture a dad working on his car in the garage. He has his son under the car with him, handing him wrenches, every now and then tightening or loosening a screw himself. The dad could get way more done without his son being there, but by doing the work with his son, their relationship is taken to a whole new level. Getting the car running again isn't even close to as important as the relationship that's formed during the process. That's how it is with God and us when we partner with Him and actually share our faith. We not only get to experience purpose in an undeniable way, but we also move closer to God through this process than we might have ever imagined.

As much as I wanted to make a difference in someone else's life, and as much as I wanted to be closer to God, I was still scared to share my faith with anyone. Maybe today on some level you are too.

So the million-dollar questions become: How do we actually use this sharing vehicle? Where do we start? What do we do? Or say?

Let's return to our conversation with the disciples. If we could ask them those questions, I think they'd smile and say, "Good questions, the answers to those we learned from the Samaritan woman that day. What she did after her interaction with Jesus was something we'll never forget!"

Then the woman left her water jar, went into town,
and told the men, "Come, see a man who told me
everything I ever did! Could this be the Messiah?"
They left the town and made their way to Him.
(John 4:28–30)

This timid woman, who figured she'd get her water at
noon because she didn't want to talk to anyone, left Jesus
and went back into town and did two things:

1. She told everyone what she had experienced.
2. She invited everyone to come experience it for
   themselves.

I think the disciples would talk about this as if they were
describing that famous pass at the homecoming football
game senior year.
   "It was unbelievable!"
   "You should have seen it!"
   She told them her story, invited them to come see Jesus,
and what happened next was crazy:

Now many Samaritans from that town believed
in Him because of what the woman said when
she testified, "He told me everything I ever did."
Therefore, when the Samaritans came to Him, they
asked Him to stay with them, and He stayed there
two days. Many more believed because of what He

said. And they told the woman, "We no longer believe because of what you said, for we have heard for ourselves and know that this really is the Savior of the world." (John 4:39–42)

She shared her story, and she invited people to see Jesus.

Because of what she did, an entire town was changed by the love of Christ. That's crazy. Countless people committed their lives to Christ. Eternities were suddenly changed, all because of one shy, broken woman who decided to share the greatest news she had ever heard.

A part of us wants this story to be our story. We want to be a part of lives being changed and people going to heaven. We want to see our loved ones experience the forgiveness we have, but our fears always seem to creep back into our minds. Here's a common broken record:

1. I just know they'll ask me a question.
2. I don't know all the answers.
3. I haven't been saved long enough.
4. I can't quote the Scriptures.
5. I still sin so I'm not good enough to do this!

Reread the story. Here's what the Samaritan woman had going against her:

- She only knew Jesus for about thirty minutes.
- She wasn't quoting Scripture.

- She wasn't winning any argument about creation.
- She didn't know how all the animals fit on the ark.
- She hadn't even moved out of her boyfriend's apartment!

In so many ways she was underqualified, but she had two pivotal things going for her: she was willing to tell others what had happened to her, and she was willing to invite others to see Jesus. Her testimony was used by God to change countless lives. "Now many Samaritans from that town believed in Him because of what the woman said when she testified" (John 4:39).

She didn't argue others into a coma. She didn't sway people's opinion because of her vast knowledge of Scriptures. She wasn't up on a box and yelling at people for sinning. She just basically admitted she didn't have all the answers, but she said, "Here's what just happened to me."

God will use your story to change people's lives if you'll let Him. We just have to be willing to share our story of faith with others and be brave enough to invite people to experience the presence of God for themselves.

Here's something to keep in mind. We don't have Jesus in the flesh, but we do have the local church. God says in Matthew 18:20, "For where two or three are gathered together in My name, I am there among them."

Every weekend when we gather in His name, He promises that His presence is with us! This is another important reason for you to find and get involved with a local church. Obviously people don't have to find God in a church building, but it's amazing how many people today will tell you that their relationship with God got started when they experienced His presence at a church service. Like the woman at the well, you too can invite people to experience the presence of God for themselves, by inviting them to your local church.

This is why I believe the local church is the hope for this world! Not because of church leaders but because of the God whose presence is there every time we gather around the name of Jesus Christ. I would argue that the local church is the greatest evangelistic tool on the planet!

Sharing our faith sounds scary, but it doesn't have to be at all.

One of the best things we could ever do for a nonbeliever is to say something like this, "I don't have all the answers, but I'll tell you what happened to me." Then invite them to your church and watch what God will do!

You will find yourself working in partnership with God, and that partnership will bring you closer to God in amazing ways. And as you start out on the open road with this sharing vehicle, just know that this method of evangelism has been working for thousands of years, and it's still working today!

Chapter 21

Worth the Risk

Remember that woman from the beginning of this section, the one who left her son on a strangers porch, jumped off of the bridge into oncoming traffic? Her name is Marty, and believe it or not, she didn't die that day. Both of her legs were crushed, and she spent a good amount of time in the hospital, but she eventually recovered. And yes, she even got her son back.

Some time later she met a lady in a parking lot. They made small talk, and the lady invited Marty to church. The lady took a risk and shared her faith with a broken, messed-up young lady. Marty reluctantly agreed to go to church. At that church service Marty experienced the presence of God for the first time in her life, and that night she gave her life to Jesus. Shortly after, to her surprise, God completely delivered her from her drug addictions.

Marty cut off affairs, quit doing drugs, and started actually raising her son. Later she went to school and got a nursing degree. Today Marty is the founder and CEO of Hospice Care of America, and one of her favorite things to do is to sit next to someone during the last days of their life, attend to their needs, and talk to them about Jesus. Marty's life was forever changed because one person took a risk on someone that everybody else had given up on.

Marty's story is special to me because Marty is my mom. I was the baby that was put in a carrier and set on a stranger's porch while my mother jumped off of a bridge. I was the two-year-old whose piggy bank would be robbed from time to time so mommy could buy heroin. But somebody took a risk. Somebody shared her faith. Somebody invited my mom to a church. Because she did, many lives have been changed forever.

See, my mom got "saved" and took me to church as a little boy, where I learned about heaven and hell. Because she did, when I was twenty-four years old and sitting at a table ready to kill myself, I couldn't because I'd learned about heaven and hell. God saved my life and healed me from a drug addiction. I became a pastor, met my wife in a small group, and have three little boys today. My nine-year-old son, Ethan, just got baptized this year and told the whole world of his faith in Jesus Christ. All because one lady in a parking lot took a risk on a heroin addict, three generations of people are going to heaven! Countless lives, including my own, have been changed by the power of God through one woman willing to take a risk and extend and invite. For that I am eternally grateful!

You can do this! You can share your faith. You can take a risk on someone that everybody else has already given up on. Tell them your story. Invite them to your church. You will experience a purpose in life that is out of this world, and you will move closer to God in a way that will amaze you. Trust me, I know from firsthand experience: it's worth the risk!

Rubber Hits the Road

Chapter 22

The Gas Is on Your Side

A ndy Stanley said, "Direction, not intention, determines destination."

Good intentions won't take you anywhere. Neither will just wanting to be closer to God. Knowledge of, and about, the spiritual vehicles discussed in this book is only the starting line. But starting lines are for starting, you don't want to stay there. You want to move past them and begin the journey. Did you hear that? The starting gun just fired. The light turned green, and now it's time to hit the road and make some forward progress.

All this may sound ridiculously obvious to you, but you'd be surprised how many people read the Bible, listen to messages about having a relationship with God, and even read books about moving closer to Him, but never actually move toward Him. Don't be that person.

A slacker's way is like a thorny hedge, but the path of the upright is a highway. (Prov. 15:19)

God wants you moving toward Him on a continual basis. You've read this book and have gained some nice momentum, but you have to keep moving. And to move you have to have action, not just thoughts of action. The car is gassed up, the bags are packed, and the only thing left to do now is get on the highway and go. Start *doing* all the things you've read about and don't get sidetracked. Just having knowledge of moving toward God won't move you toward Him.

In Matthew, Jesus finishes what many people refer to as the greatest speech ever given, with this one piece of advice:

"Therefore, everyone who hears these words of Mine and acts on them will be like a sensible man who built his house on the rock. The rain fell, the rivers rose, and the winds blew and pounded that house. Yet it didn't collapse, because its foundation was on the rock. But everyone who hears these words of Mine and doesn't act on them will be like a foolish man who built his house on the sand. The rain fell, the rivers rose, the winds blew and pounded that house, and it collapsed. And its collapse was great!" (Matt. 7:24–27)

Jesus said, "It's the doing that changes everything!" Both of the men Jesus was talking about knew the same things, listened to the same teachings, read the same books, and even memorized the same verses. But only one of them put them into practice and lived victoriously while the other one didn't do anything with his newfound knowledge, and his life completely fell apart. The message is simple: take what you've learned, get out on the highway, and start moving, going, and doing. That's when the Word of God starts changing your life. That's when you'll end up moving closer and closer into an authentic relationship with God.

James, the half brother of Jesus, put it like this: "But be doers of the word and not hearers only, deceiving yourselves" (James 1:22).

James's point is that many people not only do not do what they've learned from the Bible, but they deceive themselves into thinking they actually are doing it. It's as if James is tired of the games people play. You can read this book, underline the parts that stick out to you, and talk to people about what it takes to start moving closer to God, but if you don't actually start doing the things you've learned, none of it will help you; and worse, you won't move anywhere.

In my hometown of Wichita, Kansas, there's a racetrack known as 81 Speedway. I spent more weekends there than I'd like to admit. If you drink beer, have a mullet, and own at least two NASCAR T-shirts, then 81 Speedway is definitely your stomping grounds. I fit right in, and my dad loved taking my younger brother, Paul, and me there to watch those cars speed around the oval, dirt track.

My dad loved fast cars and loud engines. He was a speed freak who loved 81 Speedway. When we went there he would spend time in the pits with the crews talking to the drivers and getting grease on his elbows. The track was his Graceland.

One night Paul decided he wanted in on the action and joined other drivers in the "cruisers" division. The rules of the "cruisers" were simple. You take any full-sized, four-door car off the street and you've got a racecar. The math was simple: grab Grandma's Buick and sign up for the race. No racing seat belts or roll bars or even experience was needed. All you had to do to qualify was modify your car, which called for the gas pedal to be moved to the passenger's side of the car, and find someone who would control that pedal while you drove.

Just to be sure you're getting this, each car had two people in it. One drove, the other worked the gas pedal while flying around a muddy oval racetrack alongside a bunch of other drivers with little to no experience racing cars. Sounds safe, right? In every cruiser division race I saw cars crashed violently into one another, into the walls, into the barriers around the pits, and some of them even flipped over.

"Paul, are there any other qualifications for this race?" I asked him.

"You just gotta be sixteen and stupid enough to do it," he said. "Woohoo!"

Believe it or not, your spiritual life is similar to those cruisers races at 81 Speedway. God has a particular course He wants you to be on, and He has specific plans for your future. Giving your life to God is essentially putting Him in the driver's seat, but you get to control the gas pedal.

> And whenever you turn to the right or to the left, your ears will hear this command behind you: "This is the way. Walk in it." (Isa. 30:21)

In other words, God has the wheel, He'll guide your life, get you where you need to go, but you've got complete control of the gas pedal. You can move as fast as you like. It may seem strange to you, but God won't force you to move. He won't force you to make progress. He won't ever force you to take what you've learned and put it into action. He'll just quietly sit in the driver's seat and wait for you to get going. It's a cool concept because you really can move into a closer relationship with the Creator of the universe. Think of that: you really can walk, talk, and get close to God, but how fast you do that all depends on how much pressure you decide to put on that gas pedal.

You get to decide whether moving closer to God happens. If you haven't already started being intentional and consistent with each of the six spiritual vehicles in this book, it's time to hit the gas. No more good intentions and no more putting it off until tomorrow because the time is now. Step on it! Find out where God wants to take you!

Chapter 23

Under Caution

E very race fan's nemesis is the dreaded yellow caution
flag. For the uninitiated, a caution flag is like hitting
the pause button during a suspenseful movie; it's great
if you need to hit the restroom or grab something to munch
on, but if not, it's just another delay that kills the momentum of the race. All the cars slow down or stop until the
track is cleared of the debris or wreck that caused the caution flag to be waved. Boring!

Your spiritual journey might encounter some caution
flags too though. If you haven't already experienced this,
you will. Many Christ followers will tell you that there have
been times when he or she has felt so close to God it was
crazy, but those same people will also tell you that there have
been times when they felt absolutely distant from God. It's
as if the race of life has suddenly been put on hold. Make

no mistake, you're going to have all-out sprints toward God, and you'll have seasons where you feel like the caution flags are waving. What's important is to keep making forward progress and trust in the fact that God is in control of your life. Don't ever forget that He has a plan for your life, and He's guiding you even if you can't feel it at the time.

> I am sure of this, that He who started a good work
> in you will carry it on to completion until the day of
> Christ Jesus. (Phil. 1:6)

God says, "Don't worry; I'll finish what I've started in you." Clinging to that promise will be key when you have times that you just want to throw out your own caution flag and give up. Usually people start to feel hopeless and want to quit on God because of past or current mistakes. Let's dive into these two topics so that you fully understand their power and influence in your journey toward God.

Past Mistakes

I remember the week I gave my life to God. I was still in Rockford and was sitting in the sanctuary where I had committed my life to Christ. With my head in my hands, I couldn't help but cry because I didn't think I was worthy of the forgiveness, grace, and love I was experiencing from God. Not only was I aware of how unworthy I was, but I was also scared to death that I just couldn't really do it. My past was dark, my sins were many, and my failures were numerous. I'd never been good before, and I had severe doubts that I could really make a lasting change in my life.

Some of the questions that ran through my mind were: *Why would God love somebody like me? How could I ever really move closer to Him?* After all, He's perfect and I'm me. The thing I wasn't adding into any of the equations was God's grace. Grace is God giving you something you absolutely don't deserve. This grace allows each one of us sin-filled people to be forgiven of our sins, connect with God, and go to heaven for all eternity when we die. Grace is something that's hard to understand, but it's absolutely crucial to our move toward Him.

> For you are saved by grace through faith, and this is not from yourselves; it is God's gift—not from works, so that no one can boast. (Eph. 2:8–9)

Every single one of us has sinned; we've all fallen short of God's standards in one way or another. We're all broken. Picture a baseball going through a living room window at your house. As you look down at the glass on the floor, you'll notice that every piece is broken differently, but every piece is definitely broken. That's how we are as people. We're all broken in different ways, but we're all broken. As broken people, we need God's grace, and we need His free gift of salvation even though there isn't one person in history who has earned or deserves it.

That said, realize you have to allow yourself to be forgiven for all the things you've done wrong. It doesn't make sense on the surface, and you may feel guilty for a long time for the things you've done, but the truth of the Word of God always trumps our feelings.

> "I—yes, I alone—will blot out your sins for my own sake and will never think of them again." (Isa. 43:25 NLT)

> As far as the east is from the west, so far has he removed our transgressions from us. (Ps. 103:12)

> If we confess our sins, he is faithful and just and will forgive us our sins and purify us from all unrighteousness. (1 John 1:9 NIV)

God went to great lengths to make sure we understand that He forgives us and makes us perfectly righteous in His sight. I still have to remind myself of this. I screw something up, and I feel terrible even after I've repented. Such times are reminders that I have been made righteous in His sight, not because I deserve it but because of His grace and love. So I have to allow myself to be forgiven and move on. The same is true for you and for heroes of faith like Paul.

Paul was anti-Jesus Christ. In fact, as a profession, he hunted down and murdered Christians. When it comes time to make a connection with God and one's tattered past comes to mind, Paul had all of us beat! But like so many of us today, he encountered the real God, was forgiven of his sins, and then had to allow himself to embrace God's forgiveness and choose to move on. And move on he did. He went on to write much of the New Testament. He, too, had to wrap his mind around the concept of grace, forgiveness, and moving beyond a spotted past. He said it like this: "Brothers and sisters, I do not consider myself yet to have taken hold of it. But one thing I do: Forgetting what is behind and straining toward what is ahead, I press on toward the goal to win the prize for which God has called me heavenward in Christ Jesus" (Phil. 3:13–14 NIV).

Even if you don't feel forgiven, the Word of God trumps your feelings. If you've repented, you are forgiven and perfect in God's sight today. Now allow yourself to be forgiven and choose to move forward today because God has some huge plans in store for your future!

Current Mistakes

Here's the rut many people fall into when they know Jesus but fall into sin:

- I put my faith in God.

- I was forgiven for my sins.
- I received eternal salvation.
- I got fired up about my new relationship with God.
- I got excited because I've become a brand-new person.
- I started talking to God, reading the Bible, and even went to church.
- Then . . . life happens.
- I revert back to an old habit.
- I sin in a way I promised myself I never would do again.
- I just put off connecting with God for a while.
- I feel really guilty.
- I lose the motivation to connect with God because He's mad at me anyway.
- I lose interest in praying, reading the Bible, and going to church.
- I'm less likely to spend time around church people.
- I allow my guilt to fester in my mind. I wonder if I'm wasting my time and, maybe, I should give up on this whole God thing.

That was my story in the weeks after I had committed my life to Christ then relapsed into drug abuse. *Who was I kidding with this spiritual charade?* I thought. *I can't do this!*

At that moment I needed to be reminded that the grace of God that allowed me to have my sins forgiven on the day I started pursuing God was the same grace I'd need to embrace every time I screwed things up. I didn't have to earn my salvation the day I received it, and I didn't have to earn it every time I crawled back to God after making mistakes. The same is true for you today.

You don't have to pretend you're perfect, and you don't have to pretend you don't still have temptations and battles each today. When you're looking for a church to plug into, find one where people are authentic. Get into a small group or community within that church family, and be real with someone.

Knowing that you are living under the grace of the one and only living God is a guarantee that your current mistakes won't ever disqualify you from His grace. You didn't earn your way into a relationship with God, and you can't unearn your way out of it.

Depending on your personal story, you may have spent years living apart from God, so give yourself some time to be transformed by Him. You are a work in progress. Just keep moving toward Him by using the vehicles we've discussed, and if something gets in the way of your progress, realize it, repent if necessary, and keep going. Any real race fan will tell you: the caution flag is only temporary, progress may come to a halt for a short time, but before you know it, the green flag is waved again, and the race goes on.

Repent when necessary, allow yourself to be forgiven, and move on! Get back to using the vehicles you now know how to use, and start moving toward God again.

Chapter 24

Rubber to the Road

I grew up in the country outside of Wichita, Kansas, where ten–year-olds are allowed to drive. So my parents never had any of those moments where they poked their heads into my car and did a seat belt check, reminded me to use my blinkers and to leave plenty of distance between my car and the car in front of me, and to call if I had any problems whatsoever. Maybe you've experienced one of those moments or have just seen it on TV, but for the moment I'm going to play the parent.

So this is me poking my head into the window of your car one last time before you take off on your own. As I look around, I want to remind you of all the vehicles you are now prepared to operate. I'll start with prayer.

Prayer

We pray because prayer changes things, it changes us, and it brings us closer to God.

If you want some structure to begin with, use our memorization tool:

Praise
Repent
Ask
Your will
Show me

Oh yeah, make prayer a daily priority. Though it doesn't take long to talk to God, the impact it can have on you will change your life each day. Shoot for ten minutes a day, and begin lengthening that when you feel ready.

The Bible

The second vehicle, if you recall, is the Bible.

This historically accurate collection of sixty-six books is God's inspired words given directly to you to guide you through this life, to equip you for everything God has planned for you, and ultimately to bring you closer to God than you've ever been before.

If you want a rolling start, a chapter from Matthew and Proverbs each day will get you going. After you get into the habit of reading your Bible daily, I suggest you read through the entire New Testament while also making sure you read at least one Proverb every day. Obviously, these are suggested starting points. Start wherever you want; just start. Make this a daily discipline, and watch where it will take you. Make it practical: Read it, write it, do it!

One more thing, doing your Bible reading and prayer at the same time each day will increase your chances of doing both. These two vehicles need lots of attention, but they will change your life so don't let them sit around collecting dust. Both are far too valuable to you for that.

Relationships

This vehicle will never go out of style, and you should never stop using it. For the rest of your life, you should always be monitoring your relationships. You should always be plugged into a Bible-believing church and also participating in real community inside of that church. Keeping your relationships finely tuned requires lots of maintenance. So, ask yourself the tough questions:

- Is there a nonbeliever who has a large voice in my life?
- Is there a big relationship in my life that is pulling me away from God?

- Am I putting in the work to cultivate God-type relationships?
- Am I really allowing them into my life, sharing my sins, accepting prayer, and being challenged to move closer to God because of them?

If the answers aren't what they should be, then continue at every stage to be brave enough to make the right choices and make the necessary changes. The people that are close to you will impact your destination in life; it's that simple. So work hard to form strong relationships with people who will take you closer to God. For the rest of your life, you'll be glad you did.

Serving

Once you're in a local church, you need to serve in that church and in your community. The goal should be to serve people in your own world. If you want a funeral you can be proud of, one where people remember you as truly being great and generous, then you've got to start serving people today. Of course you'll try to talk yourself out of it from time to time. I do that too. We'll just have to fight off those mind games and remind ourselves that Jesus was the greatest servant ever, and thus we should be serving as well. Not only will this affect your relationship with others, but it will have a profound impact on your ever-growing relationship with God.

Giving

You'll drive this one for the rest of your life as well and will need your local church to operate it. I suggest you start giving 10 percent now to your local church, knowing it will never be easy to get started. But once you start giving, you'll see the difference it makes in your life and your pocketbook. More important than the exact percentage is just starting, so pick one you're comfortable with and be consistent and open to God calling you to higher levels of giving down the road. Remember, this is the only command God gives in the entire Bible that He follows up with, "Test Me." It's as if He is saying, "Test Me to see if I won't bless you like crazy. Watch how I'll change things about your life."

Sharing

This vehicle should be used until you take your last breath. Look for opportunities with everyone God puts in your sphere of influence to share your faith with. Get baptized—this is step one in taking your faith public. Share your testimony and invite people to church with you. The key to having an easy opportunity to share with people is to pray for and serve them. God will use your story of life-change to change other people's eternities. While doing so, He'll change you and bring you closer to Him in the process.

Let me remind you one last time. These vehicles won't make God love you more. They won't allow you to earn your salvation any more or less. God loves you just the way you are, and if you've put your trust in Him, you are saved for all of eternity. But these vehicles will give you the opportunity to move into a closer relationship with God. These vehicles will take relating to God out of the ethereal and put it into the practical. This is about really experiencing an authentic connection with God Himself, and you can do this!

Now that we've checked to be sure you're ready to hit the road, get going! You've been stuck in neutral long enough. But always keep in mind that your journey toward God will never end until heaven, which means you'll get to keep using these vehicles as long as you're around. And like a really good road trip, what you'll soon find out is that there is purpose, joy, peace, grace, and fun in the journey.

After that crazy night in front of the mirror in my Hollywood apartment, I took a long time to become aware of and start using all of the spiritual vehicles in this book. Sure, I failed at times, stopped for days here and there, failed some more; but I kept moving closer to God. I just knew it would be worth all the false starts, check engine lights, yellow flags, and missed turns.

Sometime after I made using these vehicles a habit, I returned to Hollywood to visit my roommate and great friend, Greg. When he saw me, he picked me up and bear-hugged me.

"Johnson!" he said as he set me down. "Man, you don't even look the same!"

That was the nicest thing anyone had ever said to me! Get this: I hadn't lost any weight. I hadn't changed my hairstyle. I hadn't even changed the way I dressed, but my best friend Greg could see it. I was a different person from the one he knew before. Why? Because I was using God-given spiritual vehicles that were changing my life and moving me into a closer relationship with God.

Remember the first Scripture we looked at together in the beginning of this book? "'When you come looking for me, you'll find me. Yes, when you get serious about finding me and want it more than anything else, I'll make sure you won't be disappointed.' God's Decree. 'I'll turn things around for you'" (Jer. 29:13–14 MSG).

That's it, isn't it? When we start pursuing God, He changes us in crazy ways. He turns everything in our lives so upside down that old friends can't help but notice that we are different in a good way.

You can do this! God is waiting with open arms for you, and He couldn't be more excited to have you begin moving into a real and authentic relationship with Him. This isn't about perfection; it's about effort. God is clear: you pursue Me with some effort, and I'll change everything. He's an amazing God. He loves you like crazy and can't wait to spend time with you. So go, and enjoy what will be the most exhilarating ride of your life . . . in *Transit*.

NOTES

1. Richard J. Foster, *Celebration of Discipline: The Path to Spiritual Growth* (New York, NY: HarperCollins, 1978, 1988, 1998).

2. Bill Hybels, *Too Busy Not to Pray* (Downers Grove, IL: InterVarsity Press, 1988, 1998, 2008).

3. Greg Hawkins and Cally Parkinson, *Move* (Willow Creek Association, 2001).

4. Rick Warren, *The Purpose Driven Life* (Grand Rapids, MI: Zondervan, 2002).